DEATH IS HARD
TO LIVE WITH

DEATH IS HARD TO LIVE WITH

Teenagers and How They Cope with Loss

Janet Bode

Art by Stan Mack

Delacorte Press

Published by
Delacorte Press
Bantam Doubleday Dell Publishing Group, Inc.
1540 Broadway
New York, New York 10036

Library of Congress Cataloging in Publication Data
Death is hard to live with : teenagers and how they cope with
loss / [compiled] by Janet Bode.
    p. cm.
Includes bibliographical references.
ISBN 0-385-31041-2 BT 15.95 8.68 5 94
    1. Youth and death—Case studies. 2. Death—Psychological
aspects—Case studies. 3. Bereavement—Psychological aspects
—Case studies I. Bode, Janet.
BF724.3.D43D43   1993
155.9'37'0835—dc20   92-32409
                                                          CIP
                                                           AC

Book design by Robin Arzt

Manufactured in the United States of America

September 1993

10 9 8 7 6 5 4 3 2 1

BVG

IN MEMORY OF MY FRIENDS

Janet Crane
Andy Davi
David Seibert
Nanci Wells

CONTENTS

Death Is
Not Optional

THE FACTS OF DEATH

QUESTIONING DEATH

Has a close relative or friend of yours died?
Have you ever seen a dead body?
Have you wondered, What does death feel like?
Have you attended a funeral?
Have you thought, Does a person go anywhere after
death? Why are we here, anyway?

Some of you don't want to think about death. You want to forget that everything alive must die. Plants, ants, snakes, fish, dogs, cats—and people. You want to believe that you and those you love are somehow going to live forever.

*

You read the headlines: GUNMAN KILLS 4 AT HIGH SCHOOL BE-FORE GIVING UP
FUNERAL IS HELD FOR YOUTH STRANGLED AS HE PRAYED
DESPONDENT FATHER COMMITS SUICIDE AT SITE OF SLAYING OF 16-YEAR-OLD SON

*

But they are just headlines. People around you say, "That could never happen here." And then one day it does.

*

At school you discover that over the weekend three students died when their car slammed into a wall.

Or you learn that the Cambodian immigrant in your homeroom has chilling memories of a forced march across his native land on a road littered with dead bodies.

Or you suddenly find yourself comforting your mom because her best friend died of breast cancer.

*

DEATH, LIFE, AND VIOLENCE

Each year in the United States more than two million people die. Two-thirds of them are sixty-five or over.[1] That is normal.

Now, though, there is a new "normal" to confront. In the last twenty years, while adults' death rates have gone down, the teenage mortality rate has gone up.[2]

Put simply, you're killing yourselves and each other at a record-setting pace. And the rate is soaring. No one should be blind to these facts.

Statistics show that the number-one cause of death among teens is violent injuries. About 75 percent of teenage deaths are due to one of three things: automobile accidents, suicides, and homicides.

With certain ethnic groups, the order shifts. But it's always the same three acts of violence that end teenagers' lives.

SURVIVORS

Every person who dies leaves behind survivors. No matter the cause or the age of the loved one lost, you—the survivors —hurt. The words used to console you sound artificial. How could anyone know how you feel?

You're told that the death is a "tragedy," a "release," a

"shame." You're told that death is as natural as birth. Without one there cannot be the other.

You still feel pain, rage, frustration, and a numbing sense of loss.

Soon you discover that, as individuals and as a society, we don't know how to react to a death. We don't know how to help each other ease the sorrow. We don't even know how to really talk about it.

A SURVIVAL GUIDE

This book is a place to start sorting out your emotions and making sense of your world. Think of it as a survival guide. This book will help answer the question: How do I cope with the death of someone special?

Wherever that person is, whether there's a soul, eternity, reincarnation—you're still here. How do you deal with your conflicting emotions and get on with your life?

To help you on your own journey, teenagers from across the country recount how they face these questions head on.

Leticia talks about putting her life back together after the death of her best friend, one of six students in her class to die during their senior year.

*

Sixteen-year-old Emily explains how she stopped blaming herself for her mother's death from cancer.

*

Duane, an American Indian, describes his nation's attitude toward death and the burial of his favorite uncle.

*

VIEWPOINTS ON DEATH

In their own words, in their own ways, different teenagers tell what they believe is the meaning of life. They share what they have learned about grieving, honoring the dead, and accepting the loss.

To protect their privacy, their names and a few identifying details have been changed. Their feelings and advice, as well as the other facts of their stories, remain absolutely true.

Interspersed with these chapters, adults offer their perspectives on death from practical, emotional, and philosophical viewpoints. You hear from people who deal with death on a daily basis—doctors, a police commander, a funeral director.

You also hear from people with information about why you feel the way you feel when a loved one dies. Just as important, they offer suggestions about how to defy your pain, how to move on.

In the last major section of the book, people of different beliefs speak about rituals. They, too, put death in the context of life. They, too, help you answer the eternal questions with which all of humanity struggles.

WHAT NEXT?

Whether you've been personally touched by the death of a loved one, or you're researching the topic for a paper, reading, thinking, and talking about death and violence make it easier to cope with the reality.

You don't have to read this book from start to finish. Read the titles. Skim the pages. Check out some of the boxed information. Begin where you feel the strongest connection.

For example, in brackets in the table of contents and throughout the book on the upper left side of each teenager's story is the relationship to the teenager of the person or persons who died: mother, brother, friend, and so on.

Has your mother died? Maybe accounts of a mother's death are what you want to read first.

At the top of each adult's page, his or her name and job title are given. Are you going to a Catholic funeral? You might want to find out what a priest has to say on that subject. Or you may want to find out what Jewish people do to mourn the dead.

No matter where you start or where you finish, know that:

1. You are not alone in experiencing loss.
2. There is always someone to help you survive.
3. Coming to terms with death is life-affirming.

Death on a
Daily Basis

Friend

PLAYING WITH FIRE
Eddie, Age 16

When I was running around with Clay, my dad told me, "I guarantee you, if he doesn't slow down, he is not going to last long."

My dad's a recovering alcoholic. He and his friends did drugs, too. He told me what happened to them, the ones that died. The problems the others had.

"Eddie," he said, "I love you too much to have you keep doing what you're doing."

After a while, I decided I wouldn't be able to see Clay as much. That's why I wasn't with him the night he died. Once I heard, I went out to the site to look around. I have to know what happened.

BLUE LIGHTS

Clay starts drinking early that Saturday. He likes to get high, too, smoking pot. He's been at a party at a kid's house where the parents have bought them a keg. At two in the morning Sunday, Kimberly, a girl he likes, wants him to leave with her.

He says, "No."

"Come on, let's go, let's go."

Finally he says, "Well, all right."

Clay doesn't know how to drive; Kimberly does and she has her mother's car. She's drunk, too. They go over to what we call the blue lights. In New York City by JFK Airport you can pull in and watch all the blue lights on the runway. It's neat.

A guy I work with is at a twenty-four-hour diner out there. He sees the car coming down. He tells me, "She was going a hundred miles an hour on the wrong side of the road. She hit some gravel."

You can see where they go on two wheels, then slam into the ditch. The impact flips the car four times. Even though they have on seat belts, they both fly out the window. Clay flies the farthest. His head goes into the traffic light at that corner.

"I ran over . . . to try to help them," the guy says. "Clay was so mangled into the light that I couldn't even roll him over. Then I heard the girl, moaning. Next to her, thirty-five feet away from Clay, were his shoes. Still tied. They had both come off."

BLACKOUTS

I start thinking about what I'd been doing that same night. Me and a girl were in Long Beach. That's past the airport, on the ocean. I was drunk. When I drink, I black out. That night I drove all the way home. The girl said I almost hit a car. It could have been me, not Clay.

CATCH ME

They had an open casket. Clay's dad said he wanted to show us what could happen. People put things inside it—rings, a favorite watch, pictures, notes. To make myself feel better, I wrote Clay a letter.

Dear Clay,

We sure did like to get high together. Seems like that's all we did in the eighth and ninth grade. You always had a look on your face that said, "I'm up to something. Try to catch me."

I'll never forget the time you were playing with matches and set the football field on fire. I'm like, *"Ohmigod,"* and take off—right along with you.

I remember serious things, too. Once you said, "I don't know why, but me and my dad can't get along. I care about him. I just can't tell him."

Last night I explained to your dad how you felt. He cried.

Then at the beginning of this year, for the second time I got into trouble with *my* dad. I promised him, "I'm going to quit doing drugs." And I told you.

I didn't know if I could not do drugs if I hung around with you. Someone else would say, "Oh, come on. Have some pot." The quality I liked most in you was that you respected me enough to back away. You knew I was trying to stay out of trouble.

We were still friends. We talked. But we started hanging with different people.

Clay, I can still see you walking down the hall with a smile on your face. I hope you're happy wherever you are. Could you watch me and make sure I don't screw up?

Eddie

D R E A M   S P I R I T S

For a week, week and a half, I have dreams. I'm in the backseat of that car. It isn't me, but like my spirit. I do everything right along with Clay. All the way up until he hits the traffic light. I have my arms wrapped around him, but I can't stop him from flying away.

It's been a month now and I've done some talking. I know I couldn't protect Clay. Not in my dreams, not in real life. At first I don't want to accept that. But I have to. I have to stop thinking, "Why did it happen?"

My mom and dad tell me, "Behave."

One of Mom's friends says, "If you can't behave, be careful.

"Think about the consequences.

"Think, is drinking and driving worth it?"

I ditch school to get away from all this. I go fishing by myself, but the current is so bad I can't keep a worm in the water. And, anyway, I can't stop thinking.

At first I don't blame Kimberly. I think, "Well, it could have been any of us behind that wheel." Now, though, I find out she hasn't changed. She says she doesn't need counseling. She's out every weekend drinking and driving, still.

I'm mad at Kimberly. She killed Clay.

Then I try to focus just on Clay. To me, he's not too far away. It's like a poem my dad gave me; it says, "Though you can't see or touch me, I'll be near. And if you listen with your heart, you'll hear all my love around you so soft and clear."

I miss him.

YOU ARE NOT POWERLESS

Barbara Staggers, M.D. *Director, Adolescent Medicine, Children's Hospital Medical Center of Northern California, Oakland, California*

"I'm afraid to get into a relationship. Everybody I've been involved with dies."

*

A seventeen-year-old gang leader brings together two of the largest warring gangs in the community. He tells them, "I want to retire."

They reply, "The only way you retire is if you're boxed, baby."

*

"I want to kill myself. With me dead, there'll be more food for my little brother and sister."

*

Two girls in a car run over another girl, one they think they're fighting with. It's the wrong girl. Now the friends of all the girls are fighting each other.

*

During a game, a ball player dies of a congenital heart defect. Three of his best friends go out and get seven girls pregnant. They figure that way they'll ensure their own immortality.

*

VIOLENT ZOMBIES

I see different reactions to today's violence. As with those ball players, some of you feel, "I've got to live every moment as fast as I can."

Part of this is normal teenage thinking, but it's also because the way you see it, tomorrow is not promised. Another reaction is called "acting out."

Some males turn to violence; some females to sex.

Others have a fear of life. You're petrified. You want to stay home and emotionally shut down. You are the zombies. You come to the clinic with headaches, stomachaches, chest pains. You flunk classes, get depressed. You think about dying.

Here's today's reality. This society makes sure you can get your hands on guns. Then it shows you TV shows where violence is glorified. People are killed, no big deal.

You can even watch real war on TV from your own home!

While throwing this violence at you, society says, "Now, kids, don't do these violent things." If you feel set up, you should. But you are also capable of deciding: I'm going to be better than those conflicting messages I'm being sent.

WHO DO I GO TO WHEN I'M UPSET?

How do you successfully deal with death—and violence? Make sure you have an adult in your life who is there for you. Someone you don't have to second-guess, someone who's consistent and whom you trust.

When the world is crazy, this is the person you go to for a hug. He or she is your sounding board.

If you don't have a parent who fills that role, find someone else. Create a support system.

That's why we have extended families, churches, barber shops, malls. Ask for suggestions from your school counselor, a teacher, your best friend's mom. Call a local help line.

The more you give, the more you receive.

When someone dies, you have to grieve. The only limit you should put on the grieving is that you don't hurt yourself —or someone else.

*

Find out and share *real* information about what happened. Get rid of any lies that may be circulating. Tell adults you want some crisis intervention.

*

If you deny how you feel, your emotions stay and fester. At some point, they explode. You can't be a healthy human being carrying around such pain.

*

DEATH SCHEDULE

Kids ask me, "How do you, a doctor, deal with all this dying and death?"

I say, "I believe that people are born when they're supposed to be born. They die when they're supposed to die. And I have no control over it."

That idea works for me. It doesn't work for everybody.

I challenge you to develop a philosophy, a framework of your own. You are not powerless. As you cope with death and violence you can start taking control of your life.

Start with something small. Go up to a friend who's having a hard time because somebody died. Give that person a hug.

SCHOOL VIOLENCE FELT NATIONWIDE

Several of the country's largest school districts, including Detroit, Chicago and Los Angeles, have formed specially trained school-based police forces to cope with growing violence in the schools.

[New York Newsday 2/28/92]

Friend

DEATH HURTS
Leticia, Age 17

I just graduated from high school. I feel we had a curse on
my class. Six people died. The worst was Shannon, my best
friend. She was free-spirited, the last person you'd expect to
die.

One day she's great.

The next day she's dead.

I wasn't prepared for it.

FATAL ACCIDENT

It's seven months later, and I want to tell you how Shannon died. She's walking down the street, The Boulevard, on
a sunny Saturday afternoon. A shopkeeper remembers see-
ing her. He says, "She was totally happy."

Two kids have stolen a car. Actually, Tommy, the one
driving, went to elementary school with us. He loses control
of the car, hits a group of people on the sidewalk. Shannon
gets pinned against the wall.

They don't stop. People in the neighborhood chase them.
Catch them. Shannon passes out, but then she's awake in

the ambulance, in the hospital, too. But she's bleeding internally.

At first she can talk. They ask her, "What month is it?" She doesn't know. There's brain damage.

They operate on her.

She dies.

They bring her back.

She dies again for a final time.

THE BODY

Before the funeral Shannon's father asked if I wanted to see the body. Her sisters told me, "It helps. She doesn't look at all like herself."

"No," I said, "it would be too hard for me."

MY PROTECTOR

After the funeral I cry for weeks. There are times I wish I'd seen the body. I don't believe she's dead. I think, "There's a mistake."

Memories spill through my mind night and day. Shannon and I meet in first grade. Sit next to each other. By junior high we pretend we are twins connected at the elbow. She's my protector.

Shannon is an adult from the time she is thirteen. She is independent and creative, sarcastic, but sweet. She is her own person and people respect her.

All through high school, there is Derek, this boy in her life. They are always off and on. They love each other, but he's immature. "He's always insulting me," Shannon complains.

At the time of her death, Derek's going out with somebody else. The week before, Shannon calls him and says, "Do you love me?"

Kidding, he says, "No."

Now he could *kill* himself.

THE CHANGES

I go back to the place where Shannon was hit. People leave flowers, notes, mementos. I hear, "You've got to let this go."

"I'd give my right arm to have her back," I answer.

I visit her family. They take me into her room. They keep it the same. Her sisters say, "We sleep here sometimes. It makes us feel closer to Shannon."

I have a paper due at school and I just don't want to do it. My mother goes to the library. She makes notes for me. I don't write my college essays, either.

I start smoking again.

I stop exercising, something I'd been doing every day.

I feel mad in general.

"Why are we living?" I ask my mother. "I don't know if anything has, like, a big point anymore. And if it doesn't, at least I might as well do what makes me happy."

THE PREMONITION

Tommy was found guilty at the trial. The fourteen-year-old was given probation. Shannon's mother wanted her friends to demand a harsh sentence. Do you know something? I don't blame them that much.

What they did was irresponsible. But, I mean, those boys were young, too. Kids do stupid things. They stole a car they didn't know how to drive. I can't imagine they had any intention of killing somebody.

In fact, Tommy tried to kill himself in jail. I don't think Shannon would have wanted him to be thrown away for this. She'd think he needs help. She was full of love for life.

When we were in sixth grade together Tommy wrote a little poem that was part of a class booklet. He wrote how he was alone on The Boulevard.

Nobody else was there.

Only death.

WHO'S NEXT?

People say teenagers think they're immortal. I feel I could die any minute. I wonder, "Who's next?" It seems so easy to die that it's a wonder so many of us are still alive.

Recently I made up my mind not to take people for granted and to be more careful. I no longer keep in the pain. I talk to people who knew Shannon. I'm not afraid to grieve.

Death hurts those left behind. That's what her death has taught me.

WHEN IS DEAD DEAD?

Daniel Lawlor, M.D., *Family Practice;*
President, Committee of Interns and Residents,
New York, New York

From a medical standpoint, when is a person dead? That's in dispute.

For example, in the ICU, the Intensive Care Unit, there are folks who can't talk, can't eat, can't take care of their toilet needs, can't respond to stimuli—whether verbal or physical.

*

They are hooked up to high-tech equipment with tubes down their noses, tubes to their stomachs, tubes down their throats. That's probably what's keeping them alive. Medically, though, they're not physically dead.

*

HIGH-TECH DEATH

Let's say the electroencephalogram, the EEG, the electronic means of monitoring brain activity, shows there is none. Sometimes even when the patient doesn't display any brain activity, we still keep the bloodstream flowing, the lungs going. To be crude, I think we're just keeping the organs alive.

There are laws regarding the determination of death. Before we can disconnect the life supports, before the person can be declared dead, we need the absence of brain activity along with other criteria, such as lack of normal response to an equilibrium test and carbon dioxide in the blood.

HUMAN DEATH

I was with an eighty-five-year-old woman when she died. We medicated her with morphine. She was in and out of sleep. When she was awake, she talked about her life.

Then she fell into a deep sleep. I couldn't shake her awake. Her muscles became relaxed. Her face became completely unlined, no more worry wrinkles.

Her respiration became slower and slower. She was hooked up to a cardiac monitor, the EKG, so I could observe her heart rate. It was starting to slow down, too. Finally, she took a last gasp. People call it a death rattle.

She stopped breathing, but her heart was still pumping. I watched the EKG until finally there were no more blips. She looked peaceful. I left the room to call her family. A half hour later when I came back, she was already cool to touch.

The nurse's aides came in. They gently rolled her off the bed onto a stretcher and covered her with a sheet. We all got in the elevator and went down to the morgue.

They rolled her onto a long table that goes into a refrigerator. Then they tagged her toe with her name and ID.

Friend

FOUR MUSKETEERS—MINUS ONE
Steve, Age 14

We're the Four Musketeers: me (my name's Steve), Shelby, Charlie, and David. We do all the typical kid stuff together. We have huge water-gun fights. Play sports. Have sleepovers. Go crabbing at outrageous hours of the morning just for the heck of it.

One Saturday morning four months ago Charlie calls me and says, "David—he's dead."

"What?!"

"David's dead."

I think Charlie's joking. A couple of days earlier David and I had been talking about toilet-papering a friend's house.

Charlie says, "He committed suicide last night."

We get Shelby on a conference call and that's when it first sets in. David's gone. We all feel guilty. Was there anything we could have said or done that would have changed it?

"He just didn't seem like a person who'd do this," says Charlie. "He was down-to-earth."

"Yeah," I say. "Remember when the gym teacher was going to flunk me 'cause I'd broken my leg and couldn't do any sports? David was the one who stood up to him and said, 'You can't flunk Steve.' "

YOUR OWN HELL

None of us had ever dealt with something like this before. We tried to put together a theory on why David would end his life.

David got really interested in things. It was breweries for a while, then volcanoes, next golf courses. "Maybe he got interested in death," Shelby said. "At lunch yesterday he was asking me about the movie *Flatliners*."

That was the one with the medical students, with Julia Roberts and Kiefer Sutherland. It scared me when I saw it. They took turns helping each other die, but then they all came back to life.

"David was saying stuff like, 'I've been thinking about life after death. I hear when you die you have this calm feeling.' Then he'd switch and say, 'When you die, you pick your own hell. When you come back, you can haunt whoever you want.' "

Did David think he'd be like the people in *Flatliners*? we wondered.

"I'm angry," I said. "He didn't give us or himself a chance at life."

"Why can't death just happen to people like murderers?"

"If God's so divine, why doesn't He stop it?" Charlie said.

That day we had no answers.

No Suicides

David blows a hole in his chest with his father's gun. His parents say, "It's an accident." Everything is done quickly. The police never even do an investigation. Suicides aren't supposed to happen here.

No Suckers

The viewing was right away, too, an open casket. My mom and dad dropped me off. I told them, "Ten minutes." I didn't think it would be an open casket.

For a half hour I sat in the funeral parlor to gather the nerve to see his body. When I finally went up, David didn't look real. His lips were sewn together. You could see the doctor's wounds from the autopsy.

When I came out, my dad asked, "Steve, what are you feeling right now?"

"I don't know. I'm confused."

Next was the church for the service. It was overflowing with people. David wasn't popular in going to parties, but everyone liked him.

The minister started talking about him.

"David was a brilliant kid," he began. "He wrote stories—award-winners—that you couldn't put down. He touched so many people's lives."

People were crying. "Do I cry or do I just sit here?" I wondered. Even hard-nosed Shelby had tears running down his face.

My eyes only got watery.

At the cemetery it was so cold that the wind nailed you. People put flowers on the casket. We said prayers and joined hands. Trust me, you don't want to be there when they lower the casket into the ground.

You realize, that's it. Ol' Dave is not going to pop out of there and go, "Ha, ha, suckers, fooled you!" I wanted to hear that, almost half expected it.

When I got home, I kept thinking about David. I started to cry. My parents came and sat on my bed. My dad said, "Crying helps get it out."

"Talk to us, to your friends, to your counselor," added my mom.

I went to a counselor for my grades. I'd been slacking off some. The next time I saw him, I told him what happened with David.

He tried to convince me that suicide wasn't the right thing to do. Even if my life seemed terrible, I should run away to a friend's house for a couple of days until things calmed down.

Once you pull the trigger, that's it.

QUESTION EVERYTHING

David's death causes me—causes all three of us—to question everything. "Who is this person Steve? What does he want from life?" I ask my dad.

Shelby, Charlie, and I—we're all changing. This forced us to mature. We've decided that we'll never let each other become alienated. We'll stick together.

We now look to see if one of us is down. Whenever we notice a head staring at the floor, we go, "Are you all right?"

If that doesn't satisfy us, we call. We say, "Hey, what's wrong?" We try to boost up each other so we're always on a permanent plateau.

Of course, hindsight is 20/20.

I wish David and I had done more stuff together. By coincidence we once saw *Dead Poets Society* together. *"Carpe diem*—seize the day" was the movie's philosophy. That's mine now, too.

PUSH THE ENVELOPE

Even though we still talk about David in the present tense, he no longer has a future. I want to be a fighter pilot. They have a saying, "push the envelope." You try to take your efforts as far as you can. I'd like to find out how far I can go.

In a way I think that's what David was trying to do.

CHECKERS: STEVE'S STORY

A little five-year-old friend died of cancer. Just before her death, a neighbor had a near tragedy. Her son fell off a pier and hit his head. She pulled him from the water and resuscitated him. When he came to, she asked him, "Do you remember anything?"

"Yes," he said, "there was a doorway with light coming through and inside two guys were playing checkers."

Right before our friend with cancer passed away, she woke up with a 104-degree temperature. She turned to her mother and said, "Why are they playing checkers?"

A DEAD BODY IS EVIDENCE
Captain John Carroll, 41st Precinct Commander, Bronx, New York

I had to shovel up a man who fell off the George Washington Bridge onto the pavement.

I had to tell a husband his pregnant wife had been raped and murdered. All the while I'm thinking, "Did he have anything to do with it?"

To me a dead body is the "remains," a piece of evidence.

*

KILLING AND MISSING

Once I had to shoot at a man after he shot at me and another detective. I missed and we chased him into an abandoned building. That night my teenage son said, "Retire before they kill you."

I wish more of you kids appreciated how important you are as individuals. How precious life is. Some of you think, "It's okay to kill." You even kill yourself. You think, "I'll show them for not caring about me."

Mother
Brothers
Uncle
Aunts
Cousin

NOBODY'S THERE
Jamaal, Age 13

In one year I lose seven people. My mother, my two brothers, an uncle, two aunts, and a little cousin. They die of the usual things—heart attacks, cancer, measles, violence.

I have to go to the hospital to identify my brothers' bodies. I don't want to stay home, anyway. There's yellow police tape everywhere.

Then I come to school.

"I can't take the test," I say to my teacher.

"Why not?" she asks.

"Didn't you see the news? My two brothers and the next-door neighbor were killed last night."

My teacher starts crying. Last year in front of her house gang-bangers shot her and left her for dead. She still has a slug in her lung, she says.

LIFE'S A BITCH

I can't make sense of all this. It's scary. To keep away from trouble, I try to stay low. I don't brag, don't be cocky. I keep to myself.

I don't like to think about death. But I think about all my

relatives. I have dreams where my mother's in the house, cooking and everything. I wake up and nobody's there.

Right now I'm living with my older sister and my younger brother. I ask my sister, "If you're dead, do you still feel things? You know, when your bones crack, do you feel pain?"

The Muslims say when a black man dies, he ain't really dead if he's still full of his life's pain.

I think life's a bitch.

BONES AND TEETH
ARE THE LAST TO GO
William G. Eckert, M.D., *Forensic Pathologist and Consultant, Unsolved Mysteries, Wichita, Kansas*

I don't like doing autopsies on people who die because of stupid activity. I had a kid who on a dare chugalugged a fifth of gin. His friends brought him home, laid him in bed, and the next day he was found—dead.

*

As a forensic pathologist, I do autopsies at the morgue. I'm looking at how the person died. The time of death. The time between the death and when the body was found.

With me in the lab is a man from the police, the county attorney, and a detective from the homicide division. I work with them to collect evidence.

*

I've done 25,000 autopsies in the past thirty-five years. Maybe 10 percent are on people eighteen and younger. I do a lot of SIDS—sudden infant death syndrome—cases, child abuse cases, accidents, gang shootings.

*

GOING, GOING, GONE

When a person passes away, the muscles start to stiffen. It starts at the head and moves down. Takes about twelve hours to stiffen completely.

Depending on how you die, the body turns a different color. If a person dies of asphyxia—suffocation—the body is pinkish. With a drug overdose there's white foamy material around the mouth. The skin is light red.

The hotter and more humid the weather, the more the body smells and the faster it decomposes. Gas fills it until the body looks bloated. The organs get soft. The skin starts slipping and falling off.

The bones and the teeth are the last to go. In fact, teeth are practically indestructible.

In a grave in New Orleans bodies decompose within a day or so. In the prairies of Kansas where there's no water and limited amounts of insects except beetles and flies, bodies might begin to decompose and get dehydrated. That means they become mummified. On an average, bodies decompose in two to three weeks.

LIVING DANGEROUSLY

A study of injuries and deaths in the U.S. from 1979 to 1987 shows some startling trends:

- Shooting deaths are concentrated in the West and Southeast.
- Suicide rates are highest in the West. Nevada tops the nation. Rates are highest among white males, lowest among black females.
- New Mexicans are the most dangerous drivers, with 36.7 motor-vehicle-related deaths for 100,000 population.

[*Newsweek* 9/30/91]

Father
Brother
Cousins

QUE DESCANSEN EN PAZ—MAY THEY REST IN PEACE
Isabel, Age 14

MASS MURDERER

Imagine. Julio Gonzalez murdered eighty-seven people! Some families lost five, six, seven members in the fire. We lost three. The surviving families try to help each other. Really, though, it's what's inside you that gets you through.

I live in an apartment in a quiet neighborhood in Yonkers, New York. My younger sister and I share a bedroom. The walls and rug are mint green. The furniture is pink and white. We have stuffed animals all over the room.

The problem is I'm afraid to fall asleep.

I'm afraid I'll have more dreams. In them I enter a funeral home. I see my older brother and two cousins. They're alive, but in the clothes they were buried in.

They tell me, "We miss you. Come with us."

The same thing happened when my father died. I would see him opening his eyes. He'd get out of the coffin, reach for me, tell me, "I love you, Isabel. I never want us to be apart." When he would go to hug me, I'd fall—fall in my dream.

My father died six years ago. I don't know exactly how. He was shot and left in Central Park. Now these new deaths really freak me out. They bring back memories of my dad.

CHILLS

My brother was married with two little babies. My two cousins were so sweet. They had come to the United States from Honduras a year ago. They had jobs and a future. They were all living together at my grandmother's.

My grandmother still tells me, "I feel them spiritually in this house. The light goes on in the cousins' room before I have a chance to flip the switch. Sometimes I feel a cold hand touching me. Your brother talks to me."

When I visit, I think, "It won't bother me." Then I hear knocking on the wall and I get chills.

FLAMES

My brother didn't really want to go out that night. He wanted to stay home with his wife and babies. Still, he didn't want the girls, the cousins, out alone. His wife said, "Go ahead." They left in a taxi. That's the last time she and my grandmother saw them alive.

They go to the Happy Land Social Club. To them it is a place where they can have fun, dance, and think of home. Most of the people there have just come to America.

Well, some guy, Julio Gonzalez, has a fight with his ex-girlfriend that works there. He gets jealous, mad. He goes to an Amoco station and buys a dollar's worth of gas.

To get back at her, he pours the gas inside Happy Land, takes two matches, and lights it. There are no windows and just two doors. It's a trap. Only six people survive, including the ex-girlfriend.

The next morning my grandmother calls to say that my brother and cousins never came home. My mother says, "Maybe they went to another club."

"No, you don't understand. There was a fire."

My mother starts to panic. She insists the three of them would hop from club to club.

"No," my grandmother repeats.

We get dressed and go over to her house. She is crying. By then we hear so many people have died, we have to go to a school right near the club to identify bodies. We keep hoping they won't be there.

My mother goes, my stepfather, my mother's brother, my grandmother, my brother's wife, me—we all go. Hundreds of people are there, and reporters. It's weird. We are crying, worrying, and the reporters are asking us questions.

It turns out the bodies aren't there. Instead they have Polaroid pictures of their faces. My uncle goes in for the family to look through the photos.

Other families are running out, crying. We know a lot of people who died that night. Nobody can believe it. I am thinking, "Oh, God, please don't let them be dead."

When my uncle comes out, he says, "They were there. They weren't burned from the flames. They suffocated—no air to breathe."

My grandmother faints.

We are all devastated.

Just last night the neighbor is laughing and cracking on my brother because he is fat. My brother likes to make people laugh. He works hard. And he loves his little girls. Now my brother is dead, and so are my two beautiful cousins!

GOD'S FAULT

My cousins were shipped back to Honduras to be buried. My brother we buried here next to my father. We want them near us.

Every time someone dies in my family, we set up a table in the house. We put rosaries and candles on it. We pray. This time the tears never stop.

On his bureau we keep a candle, a cross, his picture, and some memorabilia of him, his glasses, his watch. Any time we go over, we can pray or talk, like he was there. Sometimes that helps.

I didn't go to school for about two weeks. Then I went back for a day to get some work. I couldn't handle it. I started crying. I called my mother and said, "I've got to go home."

At first I wouldn't tell the people at school why I was crying. Then I just burst out with what had happened. They said, "You have to make up the work later."

I was so mad for a while I actually blamed God. When my mother said, "Let's go to church," I told her, "No."

"Why not, Isabel?"

"If there is a God why would He let this happen? Why did He let my father and my brother and my cousins die?"

"That's the way life is meant to be," she said. "Maybe

God wanted them all to be with Him. Maybe it was their time to go.''

"But maybe it wasn't."

HORSES, ZEBRAS, AND UNICORNS

We don't see much of the other families until the trial for Julio Gonzalez. He tells people, yes, he did it, but he was insane.

My mother gets angry. "That's ridiculous. He did it 'cause he was drunk and jealous." The other families agree. Some of them go every day to the trial. They comfort each other. They pray. They cry. They worry he'll get off on the insanity plea.

I can't go. They don't allow minors.

My best friend, Dilcea, and her mother help me get my feelings out. We talk. They feel what I feel. Dilcea tells me, "Your brother and cousins are in a safe place now. They won't get hurt anymore."

I begin to think, "Heaven is a place where nothing can happen to them. There are trees, flowers, and waterfalls. There are horses, zebras, and unicorns."

The people I love have a good life in heaven. And in time, I assume, we will again be with each other. Until then, they'll always be with me in my heart.

NOBODY DESERVES TO DIE

On August 20, 1991, Julio Gonzalez is found guilty. My brother's wife says, "Kill him slowly in the electric chair." I think they should punish him, but I don't believe in the death sentence. Nobody deserves to die.

On September 20th, he is sentenced—twenty-five years to life. It comes out to three and a half months for each of the eighty-seven people that died that night. My mother is there in the courtroom.

She tells me, "Everybody is happy.

"Everybody is crying.

"We will never be the same."

DEATH—MY LIFE'S WORK

Roberta Halporn, Director, Center for
Thanatology, Brooklyn, New York

Until 1900, people in the United States were fine dealing
with death. If you survived an illness, it was not medical skill.
It was in the hands of God. You died at home. You saw death
from the time you were old enough to toddle.

Then along came science. Suddenly we can treat many
diseases. We take the sick out of the house and put them in
the hospital. Small children aren't allowed to visit. Talking
about death becomes taboo.

*

IF A FAMILY MEMBER DIES

- Whatever your age, involve yourself in the funeral plans.
- Have friends or neighbors recommend a funeral director they trust. It's risky just to call somebody out of the phone book.
- There's a standard charge to pick up the body. Then the family goes to the funeral home to talk over what you want. Bring along a family friend with common sense.
- Funeral directors are not for the most part crooks, but they will try to make as much profit as they can. They know people feel guilt and are compelled to spend a lot of money on the trappings.
- You can buy a complete package or pick and choose between options. You can say, "No, we don't need that." If you can't, your friend can say it for you.

A corpse looks like nothing else. It is definitely not the person you knew before. If you see a corpse that has been what they call "cosmeticized," with lipstick, rouge, eye shadow—the works—you might get upset. But it helps you realize the person is dead.

*

A TRIBUTE

At the funeral people you haven't seen in years say, "Oh, you've grown," and, "Your mother was a wonderful lady." Put up with this. They are trying to offer a tribute that they don't know how to express.

Every religious group, every cultural group gathers the community together in some way to celebrate the passing of a soul. They support the family, express their grief, and let them know the person they all loved is honored.

Friends, too, need this outlet for their pain. It's not the same as the immediate family's pain, but they also lost somebody they cared about.

Father

THE EULOGY
Rachel, Age 18

IT'S MY FATHER'S FUNERAL AND I CAN'T CRY. I DON'T KNOW WHY.

I WANTED TO TALK TO HIM AT THE HOSPITAL. BUT HE WAS HOOKED UP TO MACHINES THAT WENT WHOOSH, WHOOSH.

HIS EYES WERE OPEN, BUT HE WAS IN A COMA. HIS BED WAS SURROUNDED BY PEOPLE.

IT LOOKED LIKE THEY WERE KEEPING HIS SPIRIT FROM LEAVING HIS BODY.

WHEN I WAS A CHILD, HE AND I WOULD TALK. ONCE HE SAID TO ME...

..."KID, TAKE A DIFFERENT PATH EACH TIME YOU GO SOMEPLACE. THAT WAY YOU'LL SEE MORE OF LIFE."

SHADY REST

TO MAKE ME LAUGH, HE'D EAT A CANDY STILL IN ITS WRAPPER.

WHEN I GOT OLDER HE THOUGHT I WAS TOO WILD. ON MY 16TH BIRTHDAY, HE GAVE ME...

...GARBAGE BAGS AND TOLD ME TO CLEAN UP MY LIFE.

WE WERE SO ANGRY WITH EACH OTHER, WE STOPPED SPEAKING.

MY FATHER WAS CHARMING, SMART, TACTLESS, EMBARRASSING.

MY MOTHER AND I KNEW ABOUT HIS GIRLFRIEND.

HE TOLD HIS EMPLOYEES THEY WERE CLOWNS. HE TOLD OUR LANDLORD HE WAS GREEDY.

HE TOLD OUR RELATIVES THEY WERE BORING. OUR RELATIVES HATED HIM.

NOW THEY'RE ALL HERE PRETENDING TO BE SAD.

THERE'S ANNOYING AUNT CELIA, WHO SAYS THAT POOR PEOPLE GET WHAT THEY DESERVE.

THE COST OF DEATH

Tom Helfenbein, Director, Helfenbein Funeral Home, Church Hill, Maryland

The phone rings. There's been a death. We ask the family for permission to embalm the body. (It's not required by law.) Then we set up a time to make the funeral arrangements.

*

Embalming is the art of disinfecting, preserving, and beautifying the body. We inject the body through an artery with formalin—the gas form of formaldehyde—and drain out the blood through a vein. This takes three to four hours.

Meanwhile we wash the body, fix the hair, and if appropriate apply makeup. I don't enjoy the smell of embalming, but I like working to get the best result. I see myself as a sculptor.

*

DEATH'S DETAILS

My job, funeral director, means I coordinate about 200 different details that must be done in order to have a funeral. First I need personal information for the death certificate, vital statistics, and the newspaper obituary—a death notice.

I write the obituary to build associations for people, so they can say, "Oh, I knew Ralph. I used to see him at the lodge hall."

The family and I talk about the funeral they'd like to have and I give them a price. That includes removal of the body, the use of the funeral home, the embalming process, the printed cards, the acknowledgment book, the hearse, and so on.

The cost of a casket goes from about $450 to $8,000. There are two kinds of caskets, the metals and the woods. Bronze is the premier, the most indestructible. Copper is half the price. There are steel caskets, too. And the harder the wood, the higher the price. They're made out of poplar, mahogany, or cherry.

Beyond the funeral home expenses, there are outside costs such as the flowers, the clergy's offering, the cemetery opening and closing the grave.

Some people want the body cremated. To do that, we take the body to a crematorium where they use extreme heat —1,600 to 1,800 degrees for two hours—to reduce the body to bone fragments. Those are then ground down into sandlike grains that weigh a total of three to nine pounds.

*

We sell tombstones, too. That's normal in a small town. In cities, it's a separate business. Tombstones—monuments—range from a couple of hundred dollars to you can imagine. My advice is to put something the person loved on that stone. Say your dad loved hunting. Carve a duck on the tombstone.

16-YEAR-OLD IS SHOT TO DEATH IN A HIGH SCHOOL IN BROOKLYN

A youth trying to help his brother in a fistfight drew a gun and opened fire in a crowded hallway of a Brooklyn high school yesterday, and the wild shots killed a 16-year-old student bystander and critically wounded a teacher who was approaching to intervene.

[New York Times 11/26/91]

MY HERO
Adam, Age 16

As soon as I see the pass to the main office, I know what it means. My dad died. In six months he's gone from digestive problems, don't worry, to liver cancer, start sweating. I walk down the hall wanting the words to drip out of my mouth: mydadhasdiedmydadhasdied.

A week earlier when the doctor calls, my mother and I pick up the phone at the same time. "I'm afraid I have more bad news," he says in that robotic way doctors talk.

I hear my mother start to breathe quickly. I'm not sure what to do. She says, "Adam, you might want to hang up."

At first I think, "No. I'm sixteen. I want to listen." But two seconds later I hang up.

I figure, "Dad's a sure-of-himself type of guy. He'll deal with the cancer." When my mom takes off for the hospital again, I don't want to ask, "Are you scared?" Instead I say, "I'm going to study for the SATs." They're the next day.

The truth is I have a new girlfriend, Marissa. With my mother always at the hospital, I'm having a great time batching it. The music is loud. I eat when I want to. I'm not supposed to have girls in the house when my parents aren't there, but, you know.

The phone rings and it's my older sister from college. She doesn't know I haven't been told that Dad's liver is not working. To be honest, I have no idea that a nonfunctioning liver is all that terminal. I think, "They hook him up to some machine." Well, there isn't any.

Something in my subconscious kicks on, saying, "You keep living your life like nothing's going to happen. Now you'll pay for it." The following morning I do the a-b-a-b thing on the SATs.

Afterwards I go to the hospital. My dad is a terrible sight, swollen hands, swollen neck, jaundiced. Suddenly it dawns on me, I'm looking at a dying man. I've never seen one before.

This nurse comes in and says, "Are you his son?" I think, "If I look like him right now, I need a good haircut."

STOP THE WORLD

The day of my dad's funeral I noticed the weather. It was drizzly and cold. I decided it should be. There's no way that someone's dad would be buried on a sunny day.

I live in a small town, maybe 20,000 people. Still, the Presbyterian church was packed. It seemed like a dignitary had died. When we drove to the cemetery, the line of cars was going forever.

That was extremely important for me. When a person you love dies, you want the world to stop for a minute. At least I thought it would help me.

But then I wondered, "Who'll argue religion with me?"

My dad was a church-oriented man. When he didn't go, he felt bad. He was what God wants, generous and gentle. Dad always said, though, "I don't want to tell you what to believe. I don't want you plagued by your father's memory, feeling hostage to it when you're an adult."

"I think organized religion screws over a lot of people," I told him.

"To thine own self be true."

"I believe in reincarnation. For the people that God considers good, but you can do better, He makes you go through it again. I think in my last life I was killed in Vietnam. Clips from the fighting disturb me."

"What about heaven and hell?" my dad asked me.

"I try not to think about going to heaven. That makes it seem like I'm only being good because there's something in it for me later."

Then we both would smile.

FLAT TIRES AND PARANOIA

In these seven months since my dad passed away, when I dream about him, often he's lecturing me. Not angrily, more giving me advice: "Adam, you shouldn't be so deeply involved with Marissa."

Even though he's gentle, I'm crying. I know I'm not going to see him when I wake up.

What's strange, too, is that he looks the way he did as a young man. He has his hair, no glasses, and is skinnier. He has the mustache he shaved off when I was ten. When I tell my mom that, she starts crying. She's forty-two years old, in good health, but I find myself wishing death on her so she'll stop hurting. I hate to see her in pain.

Plus she's paranoid now.

I say, "Hey, Mom, I'm going out." She's all over me.

"When are you going to be home?

"Where are you going?

"Who'll you be with?"

I just want to be out the door the way I've always been.

Last week we get a flat tire on one of the cars. My mom goes nuts! We have to figure out changing it step by step. Dad had done it. When I finish, though, I'm walking around about two inches taller, the ultimate man. It's nothing, really, but I hadn't known how to do it before.

Now I value my life and the lives of others around me a lot more. I've led an innocent life, and so has Marissa. Before all this happened we agreed that we wanted to try LSD. Now I panic. I think, "We can't touch that. I don't want us to die."

TOMBSTONE TALK

I create this fantasy about my dad. I'm in the living room right by the door where he'd always come in from work. I tell myself, "He'll be in any minute and we can talk about the Pirates."

When it gets really bad I go to the cemetery and talk to his tombstone. "I feel sort of jarred," I tell him. "Like I'm not in a family anymore. I'm the one responsible for Mom, not the other way around."

I tell him that aside from Marissa, the phone's stopped ringing. My friends seem to be shying away.

"I miss you, Dad, but I wouldn't talk about you that much.

It's like my friends are afraid if they spend time with me I'll be drop-dead depressing.

"You know I like to handle painful things by joking. I'd give the world to be able to mention your name in some cute way. Make fun of you a little bit. You know I wouldn't say anything derogatory.

"I guess friends feel there's nothing they can say to help or to change what's happened. And unless they know how to resurrect the dead, there's nothing I'm going to be asking from them. I suppose that makes them feel powerless. Since they can't say anything to dry my tears, they say nothing."

Dad listens.

I feel better.

On my way home, I remind myself my father's death is not going to do me in or make me feel like a vegetable unless that's what I choose to have happen.

I'm not the only teenager who's had to face the death of a parent.

Paul McCartney's mother died when he was fourteen. Look what happened to him. This guy's been one of the Beatles, is a billionaire and happily married.

I think about my future wife, maybe Marissa. I want to be to her what my dad was to my mom. Mom says, "Your dad was my hero."

FRIENDS AT FORTY

My dad once said his philosophy was that parents and children weren't supposed to be best friends until the child was in his forties. I regret not having had that opportunity to be my dad's friend.

VANISHING ACT

Don't vanish if a friend's loved one dies. Instead, bring up the subject. Say something specific like, "So, Adam, how are you handling the whole thing with your dad?" If you say, "Hey, how ya doing?" your friend doesn't know if you're talking about his dad or the C he got on his test.

If the person who's suffering lashes out and says, "Shut up. I don't want to talk about it," you've gotten the hint. At least you tried.

PEOPLE ARE DYING TO GET IN

John Caracola, General Manager, St. Michael's Cemetery, East Elmhurst, New York

---

JUDGING SOCIETY

People have buried their own for centuries. The Egyptians built pyramids, temples for the dead, five thousand years ago. There are Bible stories about Christ's tomb. You can find American Indian burial grounds across the country.

The cemetery where I work was started in 1850. There are Greek people buried here, Spanish, Italians, Ukrainians. Scott Joplin, the famous black composer, is buried here, too.

I believe you can judge a society by the way they treat their dead. If you don't have respect for any human being who once walked among you, you probably don't have it for other important things.

One night in this cemetery 848 headstones were knocked over. Then the people stole one to give to a friend for a birthday present. To me, to the families, it wasn't funny.

Death Defying

Mother

I BLAMED MYSELF
Emily, Age 16

For a long time after my mom died, I blamed myself. She had lung cancer. "If only I'd done more," I'd say to myself.

See, she was a smoker. I'd tell her, "Mom, go for a checkup."

"I just had one," she'd say, lying.

I tried tactics like leaving pamphlets around the house. It seemed to upset her. She used the excuse, "Great-Uncle Joey smoked until he was old."

After they put her in the hospital, I hurried to her room and said, "Come on, eat. You have to fight the cancer."

She was, like, *"No."* Then she busted out crying.

I visited her every day, except one. They said it was okay to get some rest, do some schoolwork. Mom hemorrhaged. They found her on the floor. They didn't know how long the blood to her brain had been blocked.

After that she would just stare into the air. People talked to her. She wouldn't answer. Finally when she did speak a little, she couldn't think of people's names. I felt sad.

I had to wonder, "Would it have made a difference if I'd been there that day?"

Afterwards my dad asked me, "Do you want to see Mom?" She was in the emergency section, hooked up to machines, having spasms and stuff. She almost vibrated.

I wanted to see her because I thought it would help. But some people said to me, "That's not how you want to remember her." I went in anyway.

I was scared to hold her hand, but it was my mom. Whatever fear I had, I had to overcome it. "You can beat it," I said to her softly again and again.

WHY MY MOM?

We didn't have a sit-down-let's-vote, but my dad explained the situation to us: She'd lost the use of the left side of her body. They were giving her drugs to kill the pain. She was a vegetable.

It was a hard decision. Still, he knew what was right. He told the doctors, "Take her off the machines."

Mom lasted less time than they expected. We were across the street, getting something to eat. By the time we were back, she was gone.

That bothered me, too, that I wasn't there to say goodbye.

She had always been there for us. She was a housewife, home, ready to run us around, to talk. She was the glue that held us together.

I kept praying that she would live, hoping for a miracle. After she died I thought, "If only I'd prayed harder. If you love somebody enough, anything can happen."

I felt mad, too. My mom was such a good person, why not have someone else die? I told myself that a person comes down to earth to serve a certain purpose. You may not always know what that is.

Mom had completed hers.

But she didn't get everything done, I'd argue. I still have two little sisters. They need attention. And what about me and Dad?

THE FAMILY STRUGGLE

It's a gradual change after all this. First, you have to accept the death. At the funeral it's okay. But when you're back home, when you try to step back into life, that's when you start thinking.

It's like Mom's on a vacation. Things get put off. She should be coming home soon.

After a while, though, you have to realize she's not returning. Talk, lots of talk, helps. We have my sisters sit down with the doctor. He answers their *what happened* thoughts. That helps settle the medical questions in their mind. I recommend it.

To deal with our new roles in the family, the struggles within ourselves, we all go to a counselor a few times. That includes my aunt. We get to bring things into the open. What we don't like. What we have to do now.

What helps most is that we learn there's not going to be something or someone to fill my mom's spot. My aunt tries to do that—to be Mom. We get upset and say, "It's not that we don't like you. But you're our aunt. That's your place."

Still, everyone in the family tries to pick up the pieces, help each other. Take shopping. I have to do it now. Other than my dad, I'm the only one with a license. I do the taking-people-where-they-need-to-go.

My friends say, "Let's go out," and I say, "It's my turn to stay home." They don't always understand. There's no one else to do these things. I have to fulfill my family's needs first.

TENSION AND PRESSURE

After my mom dies, the school counselor says, "If you ever need to talk, come in." I figure for me, I feel more comfortable talking with the gym teacher. Her parents died when she was a kid.

"There'll be times," she tells me, "when you should just be with friends. Have fun. Get your mind off things. If you don't, you can build up so much tension and pressure you make yourself sick."

That advice helps.

My best friend, Amy, is involved in a peer counselor program at school. Students are taught how to listen and how to help other students.

Amy's easy to talk to. She's supportive. She laughs with me when I tell her I've just discovered expiration dates on milk, the date stamped on the carton of when it goes bad. Before I became the family shopper, I didn't think about food spoiling. Now I'm a regular thrift shopper.

I used to have a hard time with initiative. It's scary not to have someone there to tell me to do stuff. This past year I had to learn not to procrastinate.

Before, I was a good student. Now I can't concentrate. There are times when I don't do well and I don't know why. "Am I using my mom's death as an excuse?" I wonder.

Amy asks the adult adviser about this. She tells me, "When you start to lose track with schoolwork or anything, stop and think about your mom. Your mind's already on her. Instead of fighting it, focus on it. Once you've done that for a while, go back to what you were doing."

I try that and my grades improve.

When I have a problem, I think, "How would Mom deal with it? Oh, she would tell me I should do that." She's in me. She's shown me her way, and how to think.

THIS OTHER LADY

I've got a problem now that I don't know how to solve. I don't know what my mom would say, either. My mom and dad started dating; then he went to Vietnam. He broke it off because he didn't want her to feel obligated and mourn for him if something happened.

When he came back, of course, everything was fine. She'd waited. They got married. After that they did everything hand in hand, especially following my lacrosse team.

I was so used to my mom being there with Dad. Every practice, every game, cheering us on. I decided to dedicate the games to her. That's my tribute, my love showing.

Now I turn around and there's this other lady.

She's a lacrosse fan, too. She was close to Mom. She recently separated from her husband. I think Dad needs someone, but not right now.

Me and my sisters can't understand why she calls. Maybe, we figure, a year should go by. I ask our dad, "Are you going out with her?"

He's like, "No, not really."

But I wonder, "Is she thinking differently?"

She's been married twice. She has a kid by each marriage. They're younger and we don't get along. Anything they do annoys me and my sisters. It might not be fair to them, but we don't want two more sisters. It almost seems a threat to us.

This lady comes to the house and, like my aunt says, "She's too touchy." When she talks to you, she touches your arm. "I don't go for that," my aunt says. Neither do I.

The next time she comes over I leave a newspaper clipping about my mom's death on the kitchen table.

I don't know if she gets the hint.

DESIGNING HEAVEN

How heaven is depends on you. You like the countryside? That's how it is for you. You like the city? Then that's the way you'll find it. And it's vast, I imagine.

Sometimes I wonder, "Do you go to heaven the way you look when you die?" I hope you're like you want to be, how you enjoyed life the most.

AFTERSHOCKS

Bland Maloney, A.C.S.W., Therapist, West Hartford, Connecticut

---

RAGE, GUILT, AND CONFUSION

- After a parent dies, you may feel rage. That's okay. Maybe for two years your parent was on the living room couch dying of cancer, removing any chance for you to have a normal life.
- You may feel survivor guilt. Maybe you wrongly feel by not coming home on time, by smoking pot, by doing poorly in school, you killed your parent.
- You may feel confused. Maybe your mother has died and your dad's remarrying. It's healthy for him to go on with his new life, even if it seems disloyal to you. You do have the right, the obligation, and the need to discuss it. You don't have the right to legislate who your parent hooks up with.

Father

TAKEN FOR GRANTED
Kaitlin, Age 14

*Living
is something
that each one
of us does every day.
Living
is wonderful.
Living
is taken for granted—
until it's gone.*

After my dad died, I wrote that poem. He had a heart attack at a convention in Chicago. He left about six on an August morning. He yelled "'Bye" to me, but I was too tired to get out of bed.

"I'll wake her up," I heard my mom say.

"That's okay. Let her sleep." Those were the last words I ever heard my dad speak.

ONE LAST TIME

I know this sounds stupid, but when I learned the news my first thought was, "I won't have a way to get to school." Dad drove me every day. I took that for granted, along with everything else he did for me.

I thought about the things he'd never see—getting my license, graduating, getting married, having kids. I wish I'd gotten up to hug and kiss him that one last time.

I screamed when I saw him lying in the coffin.

The pain was unbearable.

TEASE ME

A year's gone by since my dad died. He would have turned thirty-nine. He was the president of a bank here in South Carolina. Back then there was plenty of money. Sometimes now we don't have enough.

I got really sad Christmas Eve. In the middle of the night, I used to go downstairs with Dad to check out how many presents Santa left. Then Dad'd be up again at five-thirty ready to open them.

I wrote him a letter Christmas Day. I've done that other times, too. I tell him what's going on and how much I miss him. I can't imagine telling my friends about the letters. Sometimes it's hard listening to them talking about their parents.

Dad always used to tease me. I'd get mad. Right now I would do anything to have him tease me again.

THERE'S NO GOOD WAY
TO LOSE A LOVED ONE

Martin Cohen, Ph.D., Psychologist, Director,
The Life Center, Tampa, Florida

When something as big as death happens, the emotions are so powerful that your mind says *no no no*. You push your emotions back down. You tell yourself, "Don't cry. Don't yell. Don't be mad. Behave."

It's normal to feel hurt, angry, and resentful at people who've died. While they may not have done it on purpose, they have left you. Especially if parents die, your life is made more difficult by their being gone.

*

The effects of loss take a long time to get over. Don't expect to be back to normal in a couple of months. It takes one to two years for the intense stage of grief to be worked through.

*

Sometimes an entire community is touched by tragedy, for example in an earthquake, a tornado, an urban riot. Those you go to lean on are probably as devastated as you are. They may not have emotional strength left over to help you.

*

When you grieve you feel tired all the time. You're using your mental energy to hold your emotions in check. It's difficult to concentrate, to make decisions. Memory loss is common.

Give yourself the permission and the opportunity to release some of those emotions. It will help you deal with the rest of your life.

*

NUMB WITH PAIN

Everyday life is frustrating. When someone you love dies, there's more frustration. Frustration leads to anger. Anger directed at yourself is called depression.

When people are angry and depressed, they take it out on themselves. They numb the pain. Get drunk. Steal a car. Or they take it out on the people closest to them. They hurt them. The extreme of that is suicide.

To murder someone, yourself included, is an angry act.

The more you accept the fact that frustration, anger, and sadness are part of the human experience, the more you learn how to express those emotions in ways that are safe, the healthier you and our society are going to be.

Here are some physical things you can do to reduce your emotional pain and stress.

- Go into the bathroom, take the towel off the rack, and strangle it.
- Make a fist and hit a mattress, a cushion, a couch.
- Run around the block a couple of times. Stomp as you

run. Find a fallen pine cone, a tin can, a small rock and kick it as hard as you can.

• Shoot baskets. Go bowling. Dance. Have a pillow fight.

Here are creative things you can do to reduce pain and stress.

• Write a letter to the person who's died, to the doctor, to God. For that first draft of the letter, do it full speed with passion. Send it or not. What's important is to express your feelings.
• Paint or draw pictures. Take a crayon, hold it like a little kid does—in your fist—and scribble. Take Play-Doh or clay. Pound and sculpt it until you get out your emotions.
• Play your favorite instrument as loud as you can.
• Look for a silver lining in the dark cloud of death. Make a list of the lessons you are learning in tragedy.

VIOLENCE AND DEATH

The world is complicated. In the teenage years, in particular, there's a tendency to see everything in black and white.

- Either you're aggressive or you're a wimp. It's difficult to realize there are other options. For example: You can be someone who has a sword at the ready, but chooses not to draw it.
- Make your body as fit as you can.
- Learn assertiveness skills and how to protect yourself psychologically.
- Come to understand the difference between being assertive and being aggressive.
- Learn the value of peaceful solutions to problems.
- Seek out models in your neighborhood, the country, or the world of people who demonstrate alternative answers to violence.

AUSTIN PROLONGS GRIEF OVER 4 VICTIMS

Austin, Tex.—Three and a half months have passed since the night that four teen-age girls were bound, shot and set on fire in a yogurt shop, and this city still grieves.

[*New York Times* 3/23/92]

Uncle

WHY DO PEOPLE KILL
OTHER PEOPLE?
*Jeff, Age 16 **

In third grade during the spring break, I got to fly in an airplane for the first time. I was so excited. My mom and my sister, Tami, and I were going to Phoenix, Arizona. My dad's brother lived down there.

When we got there, my Uncle John met us and we stayed at his house. He was a big man, a boxer. His nickname was Stump.

I was a pest back then and thought that John hated me. I found out later the only reason he yelled was because he loved me. But when I was a child, I guess he didn't like the things I did and said. I wasn't a nice kid.

After a week we left for home on Saturday, since Tami and I had school again. On Easter Sunday we got a call. It was five A.M. I woke up and saw my mom crying. I asked my dad, "What's wrong with Mom?"

He said, "Jeff, Uncle John has been shot."

We didn't go to church that day.

---

* Unlike the rest of the teens' stories, this one is not an interview. Jeffrey Mercurio, Cedar Falls High School, Cedar Falls, Iowa, wrote this himself. He said I could use his real name.

*

He died when a friend pulled out a gun at a party. John and he got in a fight because John was sick of him coming around. When John saw the gun, he tried to fight. The bullet went in right next to his heart. The hole it made was about two-thirds of an inch in diameter.

I couldn't go to the funeral because I was too young, so my grandma thought. I had to stay home with the other "kids" in the family. My heart was broken because my mom and sister and I were the last people to see Uncle John before he died.

At the time, I didn't think his death hit me hard. Everyone else in the family was traumatized. I kept my feelings inside until I was in fifth grade. There was a story on the news: A man killed someone.

I looked at my mom and started crying. I said, "Mom, why do people kill other people?"

She started crying, too, and said, "I don't know, Jeff. They just do."

I sat on the sofa downstairs and cried some more.

Come three years after my Uncle John died, I still waited for him at Christmas. I would wait and wait and then remember, "He's not coming home again."

I feel bad that John has to remember me as the bratty kid I was. I guess I never got over his death. And I don't think anyone else in my family did, either.

IDENTITY CRISIS

Lawrence Kutner, Ph.D., author and
"Parent & Child" columnist, New York Times,
Cambridge, Massachusetts

I was eight when my father died, eighteen when my mother died. Even now, twenty years later, I still find myself thinking about it.

*

CHANGING ROLES

If you're a teenager when your parent dies, you're in a bind. You're dealing with your own identity, with changing forms of relationships. You're trying to separate from your family, to establish your own independence. And yet this family crisis is tugging you back into the fold.

You want to be more adult, but then again, you may be pushed by family members to be more adult than you want. It may not be the rate at which you're ready. There may be aspects of being adult with which you don't want to deal right now.

If one of your brothers or sisters dies, your parents may regress. They become overly protective of you. You feel like saying, "Okay, look, *I can take the bus.* You don't have to pick me up after school."

Instead, try, "Would it make you comfortable if I came home by myself, but by six o'clock?"

WARNING CAN'T SAVE GIRL FROM UTA BUS

West Valley City, Utah—Seconds before a UTA bus driver ran over and killed a 14-year-old girl Wednesday morning, he warned her: "Be careful, it's dark out there."

[*Salt Lake (Utah) Tribune* 10/24/91]

Brother

RUINED LIVES
Brook, Age 15

I was known as Roman's little sister. We went to the same schools. All the teachers knew him first.

He was special. He told you, "I want to be a rich artist. If that doesn't work, I'll just be an astronaut." Sometimes, though, he could be a mean jerk.

Roman was reckless. He dared you to do anything.

Every winter break before the accident we'd go to Colorado for vacation. This time my mom decided that Roman and I could both bring a friend along. He was seventeen that winter. I was thirteen.

The beginning of the week was a drag. The weather was so bad, we couldn't go out. Then on Friday, it was finally okay. Roman and Enrique, his friend, and me and Christine, my friend—we decided we'd all go snowmobiling.

The rental place showed us how to turn the snowmobiles on and off, and how to do the gas. They told us what areas to stay away from, and not to get too close to each other.

Roman and Enrique each had a snowmobile. Christine and I shared one; she was driving.

CHICKEN

We're fooling around when Roman starts coming straight for us. Like he's playing chicken.

Christine doesn't know what to do. She tries to turn away, but snowmobiles don't turn like cars. They skid out. Roman's still coming at us. He probably expects us to turn away. We try. His chest, I guess, hits the handlebars.

Our snowmobile tips over. I look around. I see Christine. Then I see Roman. He's just lying there . . . on his back . . . in the snow. But then, that's who he is. He could lie there and pretend to be dead.

The three of us run over and yell, *"Get up."*

He doesn't do anything.

A puddle of blood starts to surround his head.

He has a big cut over his eyebrow, a worse one under his throat. His neck seems—crooked.

"He's unconscious," Enrique says and takes off for the rental place.

Christine starts hyperventilating. She keeps saying, "It's my fault."

"No, it's my fault," I say. "If I was driving, maybe it wouldn't have happened."

Some adults come up and start pumping Roman's chest. "Is he going to be okay?" I ask.

We're hysterical.

Enrique comes back with the rental people. They make me and Christine ride our snowmobile back to the office. When we get there, they stay away from us.

My mom shows up. Enrique has called her, too.

An ambulance picks up Roman. Mom climbs in there. The

three of us follow in her Jeep. The ambulance is doing twenty miles an hour. None of the traffic is moving for it. I'm screaming, *"Please hurry."*

When we get to the hospital, they won't let us in the emergency room. "Office policy," they say.

Finally, they say, "He's dead. Sorry."

THE NIGHTMARES

At first I couldn't sleep. I kept trying to remember who said, "Let's go snowmobiling." I never could.

When I could sleep, I had the same nightmare, over and over. I'd see the accident from different points of view. First I'd see it from Roman's eyes, then from mine. Then I'd see it from up above.

WEIRD THINGS

Sometimes I feel that Roman's around. Weird things happen. One day my tape recorder begins to play—all on its own. I'm across the room. Other times something that's in a perfectly stable place falls.

Once, Mom goes out in the morning and the headlights are on on the Jeep. She starts it, afraid the battery might be run down. The windshield wipers are on and the radio starts blasting. Roman would do that; he'd leave everything on in the Jeep.

HOW COULD HE?

Sometimes I get mad at Roman.

He ruined our lives.

Our family was fine before he died.

How could he leave me behind?

I don't want to learn to be an only child.

FAMILIAR UNKNOWN

The yearbook comes out and there's a page to his memory. His friends donate a Macintosh computer to the art department. At graduation they plant a tree for him.

Lately I've been having problems. I can't pay attention. It's like I'm in another world.

I put Roman's picture on my bureau. I wear some of his clothes. I think, "I'm keeping his spirit alive."

My mom's changing, too. She's too protective. She's worried. She cries. She says, "Brook, let's both go to a psychiatrist for a while."

My first time there I yell at the therapist, "What's the use of planning my life if I might not be here tomorrow?"

She wants me to talk about my memories of the accident. "They're vivid," I say. I tell her the story again and again. It's been two years. When will I stop remembering?

"I've learned how to deal with change," I tell her. "I used to be afraid of the unknown. Now I've gotten used to it."

FINISHED BUSINESS

Since Roman died, I've decided I have to trust people more. If I don't and I die, I'll have all this hate. Or if the other person dies, I'll feel that I didn't treat them like a human being.

I try to take care of unfinished business. If I have a fight with someone, I don't leave it unresolved. I settle it.

I used to think, "I'm a strong person. I can deal with anything—even grief—by myself." I found out I couldn't. You can't. You can't do it by yourself. It's too hard. You have to find help. That's my best advice.

HOUSE FOR RENT

There are a bunch of spirits in the world. And our bodies are like houses. The spirits rent these houses for a certain amount of time. When the time is up, the spirit gets taken out of the body, whether or not people around them accept it.

MY HEART'S BEEN TORN OUT

Ellen Sanford, M.A., Coordinator,
Caring Program, Washington Home & Hospice,
Washington, D.C.

The hospice is a comfortable "resting place" for those with a disease that at this point has no cure. We also help family members deal with grief.

*

I hear, "My father and I had a horrible relationship. Now a year after his death, I want to 're-do' it."

"Your father would have forgiven you," I answer.

*

"I want to wear a sign that says, 'Please, ask me about my mother's death.' "

Your friends are afraid if they talk with you, their parent might be next.

*

Fill a box with special mementos from your mom, a scarf, a tape of her voice on an answering machine, perfume. When you're having a hard time, take out the box and think about your shared memories.

*

Just because your surviving parent is dating doesn't mean you can't keep a photo of your deceased parent in plain view.

*

DISENFRANCHISED LOSS

A disenfranchised loss is a tremendous loss to you that others don't acknowledge.

- "My biological father has never been on the scene. I wouldn't drop a tear at his death. But I loved my stepfather."
- "My dog got killed by a car. I had him for fourteen years. When I cried at school, my friends laughed."
- "When I had a miscarriage, I grieved. People didn't understand."
- Tell people how you feel.

People have different ways of grieving. Some cry with tears alone at night. (Boys are born with tear ducts, too.) Others cry with words, telling you, "My heart's been torn out."

Grandfather
Friend

CATERPILLARS, COCOONS, AND BUTTERFLIES
Brittany, Age 14

When I was little, I stayed at my grandparents' house every Saturday night. We're religious. We'd go to church Sunday morning.

Well, one year the whole family spent Memorial Day fishing and barbecuing. That night my grampa went to bed and never woke up—a heart attack.

My gramma said, "The last thing Grampa told me was yesterday had been the most fun of his entire life."

When I started crying anyway, Gramma explained, "In life, you're a caterpillar. As you die, you make a cocoon. After you die, your spirit becomes a butterfly. You never die spiritually."

I felt better. Grampa had a packed-full life.

NO APOLOGY

Last year when my friend, Trevor, committed suicide, it was a shocker. He and Danny, they were best friends, had a fight. Danny went over there to apologize and give him the money he owed.

When no one answered the door, he figured Trevor was out back fixing his car like he always did. Instead he found him hanging from a beam in the garage.

Danny could tell Trevor wasn't wholly dead. He took out his knife to cut him down, but he just got totally sick to his stomach and couldn't do anything. Ever since, he says it was his fault. He didn't cut him down in time.

"It's better this way," I said to Danny. "If Trevor had lived, he would have been paralyzed."

THE SUM OF THE PARTS

My mom asks, "Why did Trevor do it?"

"I guess little things kept adding up to one big thing," I tell her.

Trevor wanted to be a police officer. But then he was caught trespassing. He was on drugs and the cop that arrested him riled him up before he dropped him at home. His mom yelled at him. And he had just lost his girlfriend two nights before. I figure he felt nobody was there for him.

A CATCH

With my grampa, with Trevor, I hope they're in heaven. That world is a lot better than the one we're in now. If you think about the pollution, the crime, the sickness, who knows, maybe heaven is perfect. Somehow, I doubt that. I don't think anything could ever be perfect.

There's got to be a catch.

GOD'S MOVIE

When we're born, our life is like a movie to God. He can see what's going to happen, but He can't plan it. He can't interfere. What He can do, though, is give us signs that might persuade us to change.

Trevor played out his script without paying attention to God's choices.

THE GIFT

Jill Townsend, Teacher, Counselor, Mediator, Crossroads School, Santa Monica, California

Fiona had cancer. At first she said, "I'm ashamed for people to see me. I can't wear my contact lenses anymore. All my hair has fallen out. I'm skinny."

Then she smiled her radiant smile and said, "I'm trying to stay alive for Valentine's Day."

When I came to school that morning, I could tell she hadn't made it. Fiona had died. It was the day before her eighteenth birthday.

*

ACKNOWLEDGE THE LOSS

I take a bunch of students onto a balcony that overlooks an area where people gather. I say to them, "See. Everything looks the same. The lunch wagons are still there, the cars, the other students. But it *is* different. Fiona's not here. We have to acknowledge the loss."

Fiona was a gift to us. We try to find a gift in the tragedy of her death. We sit in a circle with one person talking at a time, the others acting as support. We light a candle for her.

"Fiona is just gone," I say. "Speak from the heart . . . as if she were here. Start with the words, 'I feel.' Tell her what you would like her to know."

Dierdre says, "I feel deeply hurt by her death. I'm remembering when we were on the trip to Ojai and Fiona was too sick to walk down the mountain. She asked, 'Will you carry me?'

"I have a photo of her from that day. She's on Alex's shoulders, her arms high in the air, embracing the sunset."

*

Rick recalls, "We were talking about rites of passage. How to go into adulthood, say goodbye to childhood. Fiona said, 'I cry from the pain and ask God to take me.' We gasped when she said that."

*

"Last night I had a premonition, a dream about Fiona," says another student. In it she said, 'I won't come to you during the day. You're too busy. At night, we can play together.' She looked the way she did in ninth grade."

*

THE MIRROR

I explain, "A lot of times people dream about the person. If you're open to it, I think it's a great way to stay in touch."

"I'm going to live my life for Fiona," Becky says.

"You can't live anybody's life for them," I tell her. "You can, though, live with their gift, and honor the gift. Fiona was such a great teacher for all of us. She was the mirror, reflecting us back to ourselves."

And then after all our words, we dance.
We dance
And laugh
And cry
And remember.
Fiona had been a *wonderful* dancer.

*

She may not be here, but we have all these memories. They will always be with us. That was Fiona's gift. We warmly welcome her into our lives.

When a person dies, we should acknowledge how we feel. If we're sad, we should express it. If we're outraged, we should express it.

If we embrace life, we must embrace death.

YOUNG INDIANS PRONE TO SUICIDE, STUDY FINDS

Washington, March 24 (AP)—One Indian teen-ager in six has attempted suicide, a rate four times that of other teen-agers. Indian teen-agers are twice as likely to die young as non-Indians.

[*New York Times* 3/25/92]

Aunt
Nephews
Friends

A SHOULDER FULL OF TEARS
Candy, Age 16

I collect relatives' and friends' obituaries. I keep them as a reminder. The first was my aunt and two nephews. They were living in this cute little house. My uncle went outside to start the car. While my aunt was inside trying to get the kids ready to go, the place blew up. It was a gas leak.

The next one was my friend Ginny. She looked just like Kim Basinger. She loved this guy and he got her pregnant. Then he started beating her. She'd come over here to hide and he'd follow her, screaming, "I want you back! I'll never hit you again."

Of course, he did.

When she had the baby, she said, "That's it." She wouldn't let him see her.

He went around telling everyone, "She took away my kid. I'll show her."

He broke into her house and beat her and her mother to death. The paper said he used his favorite baseball bat.

The one that hurt most was Zachary. I met him four years ago. He was like my big brother. If anybody started any trouble, Zachary stuck up for me.

He'd call me late at night, when he needed someone to talk to. We'd talk about anything. "I wish I had a girlfriend," he once told me. "If I ever get one, she leaves me. I'm going to take a knife to my throat."

"You want to ruin your life?" I answered without thinking how funny it was to say that to a person talking suicide.

A BETTER PLACE

Zachary and some friends are walking along the Missouri River, right here by Omaha. He slips and falls in. His friends don't go to the police until seven hours later. I don't know why they wait.

They have search parties to try to find him. But when it floods, the Missouri has a bad undercurrent. For a week they can't find anything. For a week that's all I think about. Finally the body washes ashore.

I throw a temper tantrum when I hear. I grab anybody in sight, hold on real tight, and give them a shoulder full of tears. My boyfriend says, "Zachary's in a better place now."

TOGETHER, ALONE

I wear a long black dress to his funeral. Usually I don't wear dresses. I feel that day it's important. Zachary always wanted to see me in a dress. I wear it for him.

To get through my sadness I decide to do things that he liked to do. It's hard, but it works. There's a restaurant, Harold's Koffee Shop, on the way out of town on Route 75. We would be the only people under fifty to go there. In Zachary's memory I drive over and order a burger and fries.

Omaha has an old section downtown that we used to go

to. I ask my boyfriend to take me, so we can just look around. I know—you know—that a friend or relative who dies wants you to go on with your life. Even if it means doing the things that you've both done together, alone.

TWO LIONS AND A DEER

I live with my mom, my stepdad, my grandmother, and my brother. He's seven. My grandmother takes care of him so my parents can both work. They have good jobs at the insurance company, Mutual of Omaha.

We live in a house with a big yard. I have a room of my own filled with pom-poms, photos, a CD player, a TV, and dolls I used to play with. On one wall I've got a huge picture of two lions jumping out of the woods at a deer. Some days I feel like that deer.

All these deaths coming together have straightened up my attitude. I was never afraid of death. Now it scares the daylights out of me.

Death seems so close.

Zachary would listen to my dream of being a doctor. He'd say, "You better learn how to like biology."

His dream was to live in a better world.

Both of us worried about ever having kids. Did we want them to have to deal with this stuff that we do? By the time they get to be our age, this place will be worse.

Where I live is a nice, safe neighborhood. Will some adult tell me what kind of world they've given us?

THE PLANE THAT FELL FROM THE SKY

Cokie Roberts, Correspondent, ABC-TV News and National Public Radio

---

NO CLOSURE

My father, Hale Boggs, was the majority leader of the U.S. House of Representatives. While he was in Alaska campaigning for another member of Congress, their small plane took off, radioed in once, then fell from the sky and disappeared.

There was a search, probably the greatest in our history. We kept thinking, "Of course they'll find the plane." But it never happened.

You feel terribly upset when there's no body over which to grieve. There's no closure. And even though I know my father is dead, always in the back of my head is this notion: Maybe Daddy's alive in some remote village unaware who he is.

I have fantasies of this man with a long, white beard crawling down the driveway, coming home. Sometimes I still feel so sad.

- Sudden death is shocking and disruptive. You can't push it aside and think everything will be fine. At the same time, you have to live your life. Later on, maybe even several years later, you may be better able to deal with it.
- After a death, some people cross the street to avoid talk-

ing to you. They worry, "What am I going to say?" They don't understand it's never wrong to say something kind. It's never wrong to show up at the house. If the family wants to be alone, there will be someone who comes to the door and tells them.

• Telling stories—laughing—is a way of remembering the person. Sometimes teenagers get angry at adults who are laughing, or the reverse. Laughter is not sacrilegious, disrespectful, or inappropriate. It helps you grieve. It helps you survive.

• The job, the grade, the outfit, whatever—things that used to seem important, aren't. After a death, you realize what really matters to you. You don't sit around thinking, "I'll do that later." There can easily be no later. It's quite a lesson.

*

Every society has burial customs. These rituals serve as an end point, a way of saying goodbye. In Washington, D.C., there's a congressional cemetery which in olden days was used as a temporary burial ground.

The people would be buried here first, then the body would be removed and sent to their home state. After this a cenotaph, a stylized marker for a tomb without a body, would be erected in this little cemetery.

*

When my mother found out about this, she had a cenotaph erected to my father and we had a ceremony. We were glad she did it.

Friend

RUSSIAN ROULETTE
Jessica, Age 15

I've lived with my grandparents since I was a baby. My dad and mom, they didn't get along. My mom said she couldn't take care of me. My dad was in the army.

Until I got to high school, I was sheltered. My grandparents were very protective. I went to church every Sunday.

Freshman year, though, *overwhelmed* me. Looking back, I figure if the first person I'd met had been a saint, I would have become one. But that wasn't the case.

MAD MAX

There I am hanging out with "drama geeks," kids that believe in vampires, werewolves, and psychic powers. Pretty soon I'm believing in them, too. We wear sunglasses and big, thick trench coats. We love it when it's dark.

I'm attracted to Max; Mad Max, everybody calls him. He's the kind of guy who likes to make you crazy. He's out of control. He always seems to be screaming at me.

I learn to yell back. One day he's really on the attack.

Finally he shouts, "Jessica, you talk like a girl that's signed her soul over to a demon."

By then I'm in a rage. I scream at him, "Fine, if that's what you think. Curses on you. I hope you die. I hope you rot in hell. I'm going to kill you myself!"

He hits me. He hits me again, but never on my face. My grandparents don't notice the bruises.

I am lost.

DITCHING AND DRUGS

Max grabs me in the hallway, says, "I'm sorry about the other day. Let's ditch. Go over to my house. I've got some coke." By then I'm doing acid; coke I've never done before. I'm curious. And there is that strong attraction.

"Okay."

He puts out a couple lines of coke on a mirror and shows me how to do it. What a rush, I think, until there's no more left.

He's hitting me again.

He rapes me.

I've never slept with him—or anyone—before. I run out the door.

OUT OF YOUR MIND

I never saw Max after that. The word was all over school: There'd been some kind of "gun accident."

His best friend, Pete, told me the real story. Three of them get roaring drunk. Max says, "We're gonna play Russian roulette." Each has his own gun. Max loads his with three bullets and three empties.

"Max had that determined look in his eye," Pete says. "If

one of them doesn't come up now, it will come up later." On the third try, Max shoots himself.

If I felt lost and confused before, this is worse. I think maybe Max felt guilty about what he did to me. If he killed himself for that reason, that makes me sad.

What he did, though, was take away my chance to ask him, like, *"Why?* Were you out of your mind?"

I'm depressed.

I have flashbacks.

I'm scared.

I can't sleep.

I can't think of a strong enough word to describe how I feel about the rape. I guess, in the end, I'm happy that Max got what he deserved.

"Am I going crazy?" I wonder.

H E L P

I fight so much with my grandmother, she says, "You're out of control. I'm sending you to a counselor."

The counselor is helping me.

CRUSHED BY LIFE

Dorothy Ferguson, *Loss and Grief Therapist, Des Moines, Iowa*

THE FRIGHTENING SUICIDE RATE

A mother calls me. Her son, Keith, died a month ago —suicide. She wants therapy for herself and her fifteen-year-old daughter, the boy's sister.

The sister says, "I don't like counselors."

"Try it once," I say, "and bring a friend."

Keith, a single suicide, leaves behind not only these two people, but other relatives, classmates, a group of nine close friends, and a girlfriend he fought with the night he died.

They're all suffering.

Adults try to explain away a teen suicide: Drugs! Dungeons & Dragons! Mötley Crüe! But it's never because of one thing. There's always a series of events leading to it.

CREATE A NEW NORMAL

Death changes the family system. The grief process is more complex with a suicide because survivors feel alone and guilty. You think it's your fault. You did something wrong. You could have prevented it.

That's not true.

People say to you, "Soon things will be back to normal."

That's not true, either.

Normal is gone now and you're going to have to create a new normal. The family is never going to be the same.

*

A father and daughter have a close relationship. The father commits suicide. Depressed, the daughter later attempts suicide, saying, "I want to be with my dad."

*

A best friend locks the garage door, turns on the car, and by the time the car runs out of gas he's dead. His surviving buddy sees death as his only option. A year later he's dead, too.

*

When there's one suicide in a family or a group of friends, there's likely to be another. This is called a "cluster." I meet with survivors to break the cycle and to discuss how to grieve a death.

*

FIVE STAGES OF GRIEF

There's a woman named Elisabeth Kübler-Ross, a leader in the field of death education. She outlined five stages of grief. The first is shock, numbness. Another is bargaining: "If only it could have been me."

Denial—refusing to believe the person died—can be a plus. You're buying time to get emotionally caught up with what's happened. Depression is another valid stage. Your energy falls as the feelings settle in. Acceptance is the last one.

These are not neat, tidy periods of time where you're in shock for a week, then move on to bargaining and so on. Also you might feel all these stages at once. The lesson is: Be aware that these emotions are normal reactions to death.

- Grieve actively. Get together with friends or family and bring photos of the person who died. Bring treasures that the person might have given you.
- Grieve appropriately. Remind each other of your own self-worth. Your value as a person here in life is beyond anything you know right now.
- Develop a routine. For example, every day write in a journal. If all you feel is, "I don't want to write in this damn thing today," write that. When everything around you seems to have changed, find things which are the same.
- Don't worry about dreams. You might dream that the person who has died is beckoning you to join him or her. This

means you miss the person. To reduce the dreams' power, find someone to listen to you describe them. If you can't find somebody, write them down to talk about later.

- Be alert to the danger signs of suicide:

  Change in sleep, appetite, energy level, or mood

  Loss of ability to concentrate

  Loss of interest in your appearance

  Start or increase in drug and/or alcohol use

  Listening to the same music over and over

  Becoming fixated on being alone, especially with items that belonged to the deceased person

---

AUTOEROTIC DEATH

Sometimes the "suicide" is a mistake. When teen males are found unclothed and hanging—people do not talk about it. No parent wants to say, "While masturbating, to increase the thrill, my son wanted to shut off the air, thinking once he reached orgasm, he'd 'wake up.' "

You don't "wake up." You die.

Father
Mother

MY REASON TO LIVE
Nicole, Age 17

My father died when I was three. My mother died when I was twelve. I didn't get a chance to say goodbye to either of them. With my dad, I was too young. With my mom, that's another story.

I was living with her and my stepfather when she started getting sick. She had AIDS. She kept going in and out of the hospital for pneumonia, for cancer, for mental problems.

One Tuesday my stepfather said, "Be prepared. I don't think she's coming back home." I was scared. He told me not to worry. My grandmother and he were going to take care of me.

He snuck me into the hospital, but my mom said to him, "Get her out of here." She didn't want me to see her like that.

MY MOTHER
When my mother died, I tried to kill myself. I took my grandmother's pills. I don't know what kind. I kept thinking, "If my mother were here, it would be different." She was strict. She would have kept me in line.

My grandmother let me do anything I wanted. She let me hang out. That's how I got pregnant. It was nothing I planned. I didn't want to be a mother.

MY SON

Now my son is three. He gives me a reason to keep going. I feel he takes my mother's place. First my mother's not there and then he's there. I feel her spirit in him. I have somebody else to love.

I keep my mother's ashes in a gold box on my dresser. Next to that I have a big, framed picture of her when she was my age, seventeen. I say to my son, "This is your grandmother."

I tell him about her, how we would go shopping for school, watch *General Hospital* together. I want him to be somebody, not some little drug dealer down on the corner. When he gets older, sees me doing things with my life, he'll do something, too. I hope.

MY STEPFATHER

My stepfather's sick now. He's dying of AIDS, too. Sometimes I look at myself and wonder, "Am I real or is life just a soap opera?" Maybe when I figure out why we're here, I can figure out why we die.

AIDS EDUCATION

Donna Futterman, M.D., Medical Director, Adolescent AIDS Clinic, Montefiore Medical Center, Bronx, New York

---

EMBARRASSMENT AND FEAR

When a family has a member die of AIDS, they can be embarrassed to talk about it. Outsiders are prejudiced and judgmental.

They think that how someone contracts AIDS matters. It doesn't. They believe that HIV can be transmitted through casual contact. They're wrong again. Fear makes people think this way.

There are support groups for kids whose family members or friends have died of HIV. If you're ready to share with others around you, find people going through the same thing.

Death Rituals
and Beliefs

Aunt

SPIRIT IN THE SMOKE
Samantha, Age 16

I'm the first in my family born in America. My mother is an engineer. My father works for IBM. We move a lot. Those first days walking into new schools are scary. I try talking to people, but they're into their groups. I keep to myself. At lunch I stay in the bathroom.

Now I go to a school in Indiana where I'm the only Filipino. Gosh, I feel different. People think I'm Asian and there's that expectation that Asians are smart. I want to be the best, but sometimes I'm not up to it.

My parents and I don't get along. When I felt sad, I called Aunt Elizabeth, Libby. I told her about school. She made fun of everything, especially guys.

"The white guys I date all have sex on their minds," I'd say.

"I went through the exact same thing," she'd say. "Of course, your mother wouldn't go out with anyone!" Aunt Libby made me laugh. When I hung up, I felt happy again.

A REBEL

Eight months ago my uncle called. "Libby passed away, a stroke," he told my mother. She was only thirty-two. I couldn't believe it. My Aunt Libby was daring, a rebel, the bad seed of the family. I loved her!

I went with my mom to the funeral parlor. We had to pick out everything. It made me nervous knowing that my Aunt Libby was there. In a refrigerator, naked, on a piece of metal. Upstairs there were caskets, caskets, caskets.

My mom cared about the locking part on the casket. I thought, "Will Aunt Libby be comfortable?" I felt the cushion to see was it going to be soft.

We selected a design, a flower, for the top of the casket. The outside was a nice mauve color, inside was lined with white cloth. We didn't care what it cost. We wanted the best for her.

After that we went to the department store to pick out a dress for her. We found a white cream with an oval neck. When we brought it back to the funeral parlor, we realized we had a problem.

The doctors had done a bad autopsy. They cut her chest up. We had to get a scarf to cover the incisions. We put on her jewelry, her rings, earrings, and her favorite necklace. Then during the viewing, somebody stole them. How could someone be so mean to take the jewelry off a dead person's body?

I tried to talk to my nephews. They're thirteen, fifteen, and sixteen. We grew up together, played together, took baths together. I knew losing a mom is hard. They were laughing. I said, "Are you okay?" They couldn't speak.

HOME, SWEETS, AND TEARS

Our Filipino tradition is to bring the body home. We have a family lot in a beautiful cemetery in a valley next to the mountains. We all get on the plane and fly there.

We have a twenty-four-hour vigil at the house where Aunt Libby grew up. People are welcome to come over, to be with her one last time. It's an open casket. I whisper, "I love you. I miss you," and then I start to cry. The way I am now. It helps to cry.

Everybody stays up all night. People bring what we call "condolence money" for the kids, my nephews. The men play a kind of game, like poker. That money goes for the kids, too.

The women cook, mostly sweets. We pop corn and mix it with caramel into a ball. We make a chewy thing, wrap it in tea leaves, and surround it with candles in front of Aunt Libby's picture.

We pray.

We're Catholic, but before we leave the house to bring the body to the cemetery, we burn a special wood. When the smoke goes up, we say that helps the spirit go to the heavens more easily. We kill a chicken. I don't know what that's for, maybe an offering.

A DOVE

At the funeral people wore white, not black, to signify purity and hope in the afterlife. The service wasn't too great, because the priest did not know what he was doing. He never even met Aunt Libby. I made a little poem. I compared her to a dove, fragile and sweet. Now she's set free.

At the cemetery a lady spoke in Ilocano, one of the many forms of Filipino. It made everyone cry, even my nephews.

My dad had been one of the people carrying the casket. Afterwards he came over to me. He said, "As I walked to where we would place the casket, I felt that it grew heavier with each step."

Then we went back to the family home. We made more food, more offerings, and more prayers. I'm glad we have these traditions to follow.

I'm scared that I don't know how to speak Ilocano. I only understand it. And some of the rituals, I don't know what's going on. I worry that I might do the wrong thing. I try to remember so I can do the exact right thing. For myself, for my family, I want to carry on these traditions.

We videotaped the entire service.

NEW LOVE

I pretend I talk to Aunt Libby. I tell her I found a wonderful Filipino boyfriend. His name is Ben. I met him two months ago when my family went to a wedding in New Jersey. We started to talk.

Once I came home he called every day. Ben's caring and honest. We don't play mind games. I tell him things I've never told my best girlfriends. We're getting to know each other emotionally, instead of this physical stuff right away.

Over Thanksgiving I saw him again. It was like, Ohhh, we clicked!

Aunt Libby would be happy for me. She'd understand my

feelings. She got married right after high school. They ran away together.

I know I'll see her again. I have questions about life, but I think there is a world after this. Everything there is not as crazy as here. It's safer.

RITUALS FOR THE LIVING

Gillian Feeley-Harnick, Ph.D., Chair,
*Anthropology Department, Johns Hopkins
University, Baltimore, Maryland*

To be prevented from having a proper funeral ritual is one of the most destructive things that can happen in a society anywhere in the world. Without honoring the dead, we cannot give birth to ancestors.

*

RITES OF PASSAGE

Anthropologists study social groups of people, rather than individuals. Humans aren't just biological beings. We're all social beings, too. Anthropologists look at how these beings interact. We study different cultures' rites of passage.

Rites of passage mark our progress through life. There are birth rituals, adolescent sexuality rituals, marriage rituals. All these can be seen as mini-deaths.

We go through a kind of "social death" and "rebirth" as a new person. Aging is a matter of re-creating ourselves.

Death affects those closest, as if we ourselves were in danger of dying. Mourning rituals help us recover from this terrible experience. They help us create a remembered person who lives on in this world.

They are the last in this series of rituals. And they are for the living. Mourning rituals are what enable the living to go on despite the death.

*

BIRTH OUT OF DEATH

A funeral changes this dangerous thing—a corpse—into an ancestor, someone who is positive and life-affirming. Together men and women have reproduced a new social being—birth out of death.

To keep that ancestor represented in life, there are other rituals: lighting candles, having shrines in the home, and so on. A shrine can be anything, a funny photograph locked away in a bedroom drawer. Or as in the island nation Madagascar, a white bowl on a shelf in the northeast corner of a house. It marks a place where death and life intersect.

AN ORDINARY EVENING
ENDS WITH 3 GIRLS SLAIN

Pasadena, Calif., March 29—The evening started as many others apparently had: with a case of beer, a bottle of whiskey, perhaps some drugs. The six high school students often partied together at Katherine Macaulay's gated home overlooking a manicured golf course in an exclusive neighborhood.

But by the end of the evening, three girls had been shot dead at point-blank range with a 12-gauge pump shotgun and two boys had fled to Oregon in a Mercedes-Benz. A third stayed behind, promising to cover them.

[New York Times 3/30/91]

Friend

SOME DIE SOONER
Tinnessa, Age 18

A student came bursting into class saying, "Hey, guess what? Lizette's terminally ill. She might not make it to graduation!"

"You jerk! You announce it like it's some ball game score!" I couldn't believe what I was hearing. I'd been a buddy of Lizette's since seventh grade.

When Lizette found out we all knew, she was upset. She wanted to be treated like everyone else.

A BUMMER

I don't know how I'd react in her situation. I guess I'd be scared, angry, and disappointed. Disappointed that I might die and not get to—life. I don't know how many other people I'd tell. I wouldn't want them to "ohh" and "ahh" about it.

Something changed in all of us because of Lizette. The fears we'd been having about graduating, what came next, everybody had them. Not just me. But what she was going through was different.

"What do you know about leukemia?" I asked a friend of mine, a nurse.

"It's a bummer," she said.

Lizette didn't deserve this. She was always smiling. You could trust her. Now she kept getting worse. I remember one night sitting on my bed praying they'd come up with a miracle cure.

FOR THE BEST

It's first period and Mr. Arthur's fifteen minutes late. We're joking around, wondering if we should walk. Then he comes in with this grave look on his face.

"Something horrible has happened. Lizette died."

I don't hear what else he says. I just get up and leave. I find my friend in his car in the parking lot. I knock on the window. He opens it. I try to say something and the words are caught in my throat.

Even after I say it, I don't believe it.

There's an announcement over the PA. A school assembly. They get us together to tell us what happened. Lizette died at five A.M. She had been in a coma for a week. "It's for the best," they say.

"For the best"—what a stupid thing to say.

Her close friends gather in a classroom. I learn about parts of her that I hadn't known before. I try to cry, but I can't. I can't forgive myself for Lizette's death.

MY OWN RITUAL

I live with my nine-year-old sister, and my mom, and my dad. My parents and I don't have that great a relationship.

That night I'm at dinner, answering in monosyllables. My mom gets angry.

I explode. "A friend died today!"

"Who was it? Tell me about it."

"I don't want to discuss it!" I scream at her as I walk out the door. Whenever I tell her anything, I find out everyone knows. She has the power to hurt me. I can't trust her.

I go down to the beach. By myself. I light a candle. Lizette loved the beach. This is my way of honoring her. As I talk to her, my emotions cycle. "Why you, Lizette? Why not somebody else? Why not me, in fact?"

"Why are we here?" I wonder. As far as I can see, there are no big glowing words up in the sky that give us any clues. Is Lizette's death a reminder how little imprint each of us makes? We come and then pass on. We all die; some just die sooner.

I want to believe that Lizette's happy in heaven. But, overall, I'm an agnostic. I don't see any facts that stand up to prove the existence of God, heaven, hell, a life ever after.

People say, "It's all in the Bible."

I say, "Who wrote it and when?" If an angel appeared floating in front of my face, I'd say, "Okay, now I'm a believer." I'd like to believe, but I won't let myself.

LAST MEMORY

I don't go to Lizette's funeral. For my last memory I don't want an image of her body without her in it. I want to keep her the way she was.

For me it's the right decision.

I won't visit the cemetery for the same reason. It's a place with a bunch of dead bodies. It wouldn't be like visiting her.

TRUST

Lizette didn't make it to graduation. She was a week short. Her family accepted a diploma for her.

While the speakers talked, I evaluated myself. I've changed since all this started happening. When I first heard Lizette was sick, in her honor I stopped smoking pot. Sometimes I'm with friends and they light up. It's hard. I think, "Well, should I?" If I do, I would be devaluing her memory.

Before Lizette became sick, I wouldn't have been able to talk about my feelings. Now I'm more open and willing to do things for other people. I decided to trust them, not worry whether I'll be betrayed.

GOD DIDN'T DO IT

Father John Murray, *Pastor, St. Mary's Parish Church, Annapolis, Maryland*

We Catholics make a big thing of God's will. We want to do God's will. Unfortunately sometimes when a person dies, people say, "It's God's will."

They get mad. "Why did God do this?"

"God didn't do it," I say. "We die because we have cancer, a drunken driver hits us, whatever. It may be in God's overall plan, but He didn't will someone in our life to die at this time."

*

THE WAKE

The night before a burial, Catholics often hold what is called a vigil or a wake. Next to the casket is a kneeler. We kneel on that and say what we feel is appropriate, maybe a prayer, a Hail Mary, an Our Father, or words we make up on our own.

Then we step back to speak to the family and our friends. We might want to hug each other.

The Irish have a great expression: "I'm sorry for your troubles." From my experience even though no one remembers what anyone says, something like that is fine. Don't be afraid. Don't try to put a meaning on death. Just be present.

The funeral the following day includes a Mass. The priest and often a member or two of the family speak. We have readings from the Bible. We pray for the deceased, for those who mourn, for those who are suffering. Later there's a graveyard service that lasts three or four minutes.

Catholics believe there is life after death. The soul separates from the body. The lifeless body is committed to the earth. Then there is a judgment by God the Father on how we lived this life. How we followed the Ten Commandments. How we comforted the sorrowing. How we fed the hungry. How we treated other people.

In other words, we are judged on our relationship with God and our relationship with those around us.

Catholics believe that in the afterlife there are three alternatives: eternal punishment in hell, eternal reward in heaven, or a temporary state—purgatory—for those who first have to be freed from selfishness and sinfulness before they can go on to heaven.

Will we be reunited with our family in the afterlife? I don't know. It's a mystery. What I know, what Catholics believe, is that for God's faithful people there is resurrection from the dead.

Mother

TRIUMPH
Timothy, Age 16

I'm about nine when my mother starts getting sick. It's asthma. She wakes up every night, wheezing and coughing. Every night I sit on my bed listening for her to call for help.

Last Thanksgiving she almost dies in my brother's arms. She runs outside for air. We take off out the door after her. She passes out. I catch her. We bring her inside and lay her down.

We get used to the routine: Call the ambulance, get the oxygen tanks, flag down the emergency crew.

Her pulse stops and starts and stops and starts. Usually they don't know what to do with Mom. They give her medicine, cross their fingers, and hope it does something. Once they call us up and announce she's dead. But she's not.

My mother tells me, "Timothy, it's mind over matter."

She pushes us to do the right thing. She keeps everyone together. She's brave. She makes me proud.

Constantly she tries to get up and do stuff for us. Once we come home from school and she's covered the kitchen counter with homemade cookies. Mostly, though, she spends time on the couch. Her lungs collapse a lot, too.

When she dies, they say, "Only a quarter of one lung was working."

My dad's job doesn't have any medical insurance.

We can't afford insurance on our own.

Besides food, the rest of our money goes for doctor's bills.

We can't pay the mortgage. We almost have the house paid for when the bank takes it.

I'm sixteen now. I sleep on a mattress on the floor of a rented apartment. That's the only furniture in the room.

We have no money for a headstone for my mom's grave.

MOM'S CASKET

My big brother shows up at the funeral. He has been working in Arkansas and didn't get to see Mom for a year. He's crying, "I want to carry her casket—by myself." We let him load her in the car.

When we get to the graveyard, they say, "You can't carry her alone."

Afterwards we have a get-together. It's mainly my dad's side. They're like him. They start talking about beer and all that. My dad, one minute he's sad, the next he's laughing. I don't want to be part of it.

"You're old enough to know better," I tell him. "The beer affects you."

MOM'S MESSAGE

Everyone leaves; we open my mom's Bible. She was a religious person. (I try going to church, but the other kids make fun of me. My clothes aren't good enough.)

Inside the Bible are letters. She writes that we have to

accept her death. She loves us. She says, "Don't fight. Stay close together." And she writes about her hopes for us.

I have just gotten a scholarship to go to art school. My mom says, "Keep a head on your shoulders, Timothy, and follow your artistic abilities. You know you can look at something and draw it perfect, like the time you did a picture of Jesus for me." I smile. Even I had been shocked. I didn't think I could draw like that.

"I know you'll make it," she writes.

DAD'S APOLOGY

In reality, at first we argue. The house is messy; nothing gets cleaned up. Dad gets grumpy. Then me and my brother do start cleaning. But my dad wants it at the snap of his fingers.

I tell him, "I'll clean the bathroom when I finish the dishes."

He gets out of his chair and tries to smack me. I block it. That's the first time that's happened. Later that night when he's going to sleep, he says, "Goodnight, boys."

To him that means "I'm sorry."

He's never been able to say those words. My mom was always the one who said that, even if it wasn't her fault.

I turn and say, "I'm sorry, too, Dad."

We only have two dollars between us. We are more scared about money than the day of the funeral. My mom had been drawing an income from the state. That was one check. My dad works minimum wage; but that's another check. Now with her gone, there is less money.

I drop out of school.

I get a job. I try to figure whether I'm right or wrong for walking away from the art school scholarship. I write my mom a letter, explaining.

I say, "Dad's trying his best. I can't blame him. I can't blame you. You're so good. I truly believe the good die young because they grow up quicker. For the family, I'm going to settle down and be responsible."

That night I dream my mom reads my letter. She cries. Writing my feelings is the only way I can get them out of my head.

MY TEARS

My mom shared things with me before she died. She talked to me about real life. "Find someone from Social Services. They'll tell how to get things with or without money."

The social worker shows us where to sign up for food stamps to tide us over. We go there and get them. Then I learn about low-income housing. The apartment we rent now is based on how much money my dad makes.

I know I need school, too. For now, though, I go to an alternative high school. I have half a day of classes and half a day of work. I split my paycheck with my younger brother.

When my mom died, she was writing a book. It's about her life. She'd been in and out of foster homes most of her youth. When she married my dad, she said, "This family is going to stay together."

On the last page, she writes, "Soon, I'll no longer be hurting. I'll be *safe* in God's hands—better off than where I am. Anyway, I'll *see* you later!''

She calls her book *Triumph.*

Reading it stops my crying.

LIFE—NOT DEATH—IS OF PRIMARY IMPORTANCE

Rabbi Balfour Brickner, Senior Rabbi, Emeritus, Stephen Wise Free Synagogue, New York, New York

In Judaism our life on this earth is held in reverence. Judaism wants us to be the best living person we can be, recognizing that at some point we die.

*

Jewish people get the body in the ground, mourn the loss, retain the memory, then pick ourselves up and keep on going. The quicker the better.

*

Nontraditional Judaism allows for cremation, but more often there is a simple burial. We don't believe in elaborate caskets that try to keep the worms from getting in.

Instead we use a plain wooden casket. Then at the cemetery the family is instructed to throw earth on it. That's important. The family has to experience the finality of death.

*

The last thing we do is say kaddish, a special prayer for the dead that recognizes the greatness of God.

*

TEARS AND TALK

After we bury a Jew, we come back to the house and do what is called sitting shiva. A full shiva is seven days. People come. Every time somebody walks in the door, we break out in tears all over again. We have to talk about the person who's dead.

A new image begins to form, a mental image, a spiritual image of the person. There is no denial of death. In fact, the refusal to deny death is what enhances the beauty of life.

At the end of the shiva period, we're not healed, but we are so wiped out that we want to go back to work, to school.

---

*

In Judaism, the heaven and hell we have are right here on earth. We do, though, fantasize and romanticize about a mythical dimension, a place after death.

*

I think the most beautiful image of heaven is the idea that when we die, we go to the Academy on High. We sit with the greatest rabbinic scholars, and all the questions that weren't answered on earth are answered there.

For us, there is no hell, no idea of punishment, no damnation for sin.

*

THE BARGAIN

A rebbe once went to God and demanded, "Stop death."

God said, "Sure, I'll be glad to stop death. But when I do that, no child will be born, no bird will be hatched, no fruit will ripen. . . ."

"Never mind," said the rebbe.

Friend
Uncle

STEPS TO THE OTHER SIDE
Duane, Age 15

DEATH EDUCATION

I'm an American Indian. In most Indian religions to speak of death and the dead is just not done. It brings on bad karma. I'm talking to you to help educate others. Still there are certain rituals I can't discuss.

In our Pueblo, religion is a mix of Indian ceremonies and Catholicism. My grandmother is a medicine woman. My uncle is a holy man.

Religion is important. I must hold it in high regard. If I don't, everyone gets on my case. In our house we keep things that have religious significance—eagle feathers, rough-cut turquoise, cornmeal. Cornmeal signifies life and prosperity.

I keep cornmeal in my room, too, between my Ziggy Marley and Hammer posters. I also have some in my medicine bag in my jacket pocket.

FAMILY AND FRIENDS

I've had friends die. Frank rolled his car on the way home from a birthday party. Another guy was shot in the back by the police.

I've had relatives die, too. One of my father's brothers, Bob, passed away about six months ago. He was a fun-loving, spontaneous person, and prone to alcohol.

BACKWARD AND FORWARD

When a person dies, we take down all the pictures in the house. We cover the mirrors. Artificial stuff like electric clocks is put away.

With Uncle Bob we dress him in brand-new Indian clothes that are specially made for him. We put them on backward. That means his shirt and pants are on backward. His left shoe is on the right foot, the right shoe on the left foot, and so on.

We cover his face with cloth, something you can kind of see through. Then Uncle Bob's laid out in the middle of my grandmother's house.

All the family members and friends come over. For the first of the next four days there's a vigil. A relative has to be awake by the body at all times. There are candles in the room.

The soul doesn't start to leave the body until those four days go by. During that time any baby still toddling is in danger. We keep holy ashes on my youngest sister's hands and face or else my uncle's soul will take her with him.

Unless you're too young or you've got something seriously wrong, you get on your knees and pray. We say four rosaries a day. We only talk about good things. We remember the person for his best. We can't get mad. We cannot let any bad thoughts in our heads.

And we eat. The family feeds whoever comes over as many times as they want. For Uncle Bob's funeral we use 685 loaves of bread. I swear I watch people bring in carloads of food—beans, chili, potato salad—and we have nothing left.

FREEING THE SPIRIT

Before dawn on the fourth day, we wrap the body in a blanket, tie it with belts, and place it on a ladder instead of in a coffin.

We carry Uncle Bob to the cemetery and bury him with things that he prizes: his amazing jewelry, and, of course, eagle feathers, cornmeal, and things that have medicinal value. The family and other people from the pueblo bring these things that the person will need in the Other Life.

After we bury the person, we can't visit the gravesite until the next All Souls' Day, November 1st.

It has to rain, too.

The spirit isn't free until it rains.

If we go anywhere near the grave before those two things happen, we're in trouble.

On All Souls' Day we go to the cemetery to call on all our relatives' graves and feed them. Because the person isn't actually dead, he still needs nourishment. We make special food, including a pudding.

For Uncle Bob we take him that and a miniature of Jack Daniel's, his favorite. We pour it on his grave and the food we leave in bowls. After the site is blessed, the medicine women and holy men come back to our house.

THE OTHER SIDE

We believe there are two sides to life: the way we look at it, and the way people who have died look at it. When we die, we go to the Other Side. There everything is backwards from the way it is here.

There everything is plentiful and cheerful. It's similar to Christian heaven, but not quite the same. I believe it's more a state of being than an actual place.

DEATH IS NOT THE END
Bishop Woody Whitlock, Church of Jesus
Christ of Latter-day Saints (Mormon), Salt Lake
City, Utah

One of our leaders says, "I don't fear death. It's just a revolving door to another world. I only worry about getting stuck in between."

*

For LDS the sting of death is taken away by the understanding that death is a transition. Families are reunited on the other side in the spirit world.

*

When a person dies, we believe the spirit leaves the body and goes on to the world beyond a veil that we can't penetrate with our vision.

*

We believe that we had an existence as spirits previous to this one. We looked rather like we do now, but in a body that was more refined. We had an ability to move, communicate, and think.

*

ETERNAL PROGRESSION

Life is an eternal progression. There comes a time when the spirit is born into a body on earth. We then experience pain and pleasure, joy and sorrow. We learn lessons. When we die, the spirit once more departs on its journey.

After death there is a separation into one of two types. If we cared about others, if we tried to be morally right, our spirit is ushered into that place beyond death where it's light and friendly.

If we were self-centered, mean, and did bad stuff, our spirit travels into a realm of darkness and anguish. We are made painfully aware of the pain we've caused others. We stay there until we sincerely regret the way we chose to live during that lifetime.

WHITE ROBES

In the LDS religion when we are baptized and married, we wear a white robe. That clothing is special. When a person dies, instead of being dressed for the burial in a suit or a dress, he or she is clothed in this robe.

GANG STRIFE CLAIMS INNOCENT BOY

A 17-year-old Southeast Asian immigrant died in his mother's arms and three others were wounded in a shooting that police described as the latest incident in an escalating war between Cambodian and Latino gang members in Long Beach [California].

[*Los Angeles Times* 4/10/91]

Friends

NEIGHBORHOOD SPIRITS
Vince, Age 23

THE DYING STARTED AROUND THE TIME DRUGS CAME INTO THE NEIGHBORHOOD.

THAT'S WHEN I STARTED DOING MY MURALS. LISA WAS MY FRIEND. SHE WAS 17 WHEN...

...SHE ASKED ME TO PAINT CLOUDS ON HER BEDROOM CEILING BECAUSE, SHE SAID, "SOMEDAY I WILL BE GOING UP THERE."

BUT HIS SOUL WAS A DEMON. HIS MOTHER THREW PAINT ON HIS IMAGE BECAUSE HIS SPIRIT HAUNTED HER DREAMS.

NOW MY MEMORIALS ARE ALL AROUND THIS NEIGHBORHOOD. FOR US THE CEMETERIES ARE TOO FAR AWAY. THE SPIRITS LIVE RIGHT HERE.

TONY, WHO SHOT HIMSELF.
SONJA, SHOT BY HER BOYFRIEND.
TRISH, DEAD OF A BRAIN TUMOR.
RUBEN, DEAD FROM AN OVERDOSE.
TWO LITTLE KIDS KILLED BY A FIRE.
FERNIE, DEAD FROM STAB WOUNDS.
ANGEL, DIED IN A POLICE STATION.

DEATH IS THE DOOR
TO PARADISE

Imām Mubasher Ahmad, Missionary, Ahmadiyya Movement in Islam, Baltimore, Maryland

---

GOD'S GIFT

Muslims believe that life is a gift from God. God gives it to us and God takes it back. Death is the door through which we step into paradise.

Paradise is a spiritual, not a physical, place. Muslims believe in spiritual resurrection. Our soul is given another form which reflects our actions on earth.

If we have been pious and tried to live a good life, our soul will live forever in paradise in the presence of God.

Those who commit sins and tread upon others' lives have to stand accountable. They go to hell, but it's a temporary location, like going to a hospital to get cured of a disease.

We are children of this forgiving God. Eventually we all return to Him. With these reassurances, we know there is nothing dreadful about death.

Once a person dies, there's a verse from the Qur'ān which we read out loud to remind us that we're going back to the most loving God. To prepare for the funeral is simple. The body is washed, perfumed, and wrapped in a particular way in plain, white sheets.

*

Within three days, the body—the physical element—has to be buried. (Muslims are never cremated. Whatever is undesirable for a living person, burning, should not be done to a person who is dead.)

*

At the funeral, there's no sermon, nobody goes over the life history of the person. Instead there is a funeral prayer. This time everybody prays silently for the person who has died, for his spiritual uplift, for his forgiveness, and for the forgiveness of those who are living.

This can be done in a mosque—that's like a church or synagogue—in a funeral home, or at the gravesite. The people stand shoulder to shoulder in rows of odd numbers.

*

Those left behind feel the pain of the death. Still, the expression of it has to be controlled. Weeping loudly is discouraged.

Women are not prohibited from attending the funeral, but because they are more tenderhearted and likely to break down, their presence is not considered desirable.

*

GOING ON

Patience is a sign of the faith. The family should go back into life as soon as possible. The separation is temporary. We trust in the continuity of life.

Community members come to the home of the bereaved family. We give our condolences, our sympathy, and our reassurances.

Grandfather
Friend

COLOR MY DAYS BLACK
Margarita, Age 15

My grandfather, *mi abuelo,* was still alive when we got to Mexico for Christmas vacation. My mom and I had gone from Dallas to Laredo and across the border to his home, about seventeen hours altogether.

"It's my fifteenth birthday," I kept thinking. "I'm supposed to blossom into womanhood today and I'm doing my blossoming on a bus!"

My best friend, Teresa, got to have a wonderful *quinceañero.* That's a celebration a Mexican girl goes through when she passes from childhood to adulthood. Like a sweet sixteen. There's a Mass and then a reception where you have dinner, then do these waltzes that you have been practicing.

When Teresa asked me to be in hers, I agreed. In July we started practicing twice a week. My first time there I noticed Caesar. He was cute, medium-skinned, and had amazing dark brown eyes. He had a quality that made him stand out.

"I want to get to know him," I thought to myself. I was sorry Teresa didn't assign him my partner for the waltzes.

Instead she confessed to me, "I'm going after Caesar."

I was crushed. I could only pursue him if I was willing to damage our friendship. I kept my feelings for him hidden.

Still I counted the days between practice. Caesar would sit next to me, flirt with me. By the *quinceañero*, I was stressed out trying not to respond to him.

CAESAR—DRUNK WITH PASSION

Teresa and her partner look wonderful dressed completely in white. The other girls and I wear lilac dresses and have white lace umbrellas. Caesar and the guys have lilac cummerbunds and handkerchiefs and carry canes.

After dinner all of us form a horseshoe around Teresa and her partner. As the cameras click, we perform the waltzes we practiced. Afterwards the deejay asks us to start the first dance. At ten o'clock everyone toasts the birthday girl and *my* life takes a major change: I go out into the lobby and there's Caesar, drinking beer. He comes up and starts flirting.

I write in my diary, "My heart melts under his gaze."

He gets this sweet, serious look and teases, "Space aliens are coming. I'll protect you. Come into the broom closet with me."

"I'll take my chances with the aliens," I tell him.

Sonia, my cousin, comes up and says, "We've got to go back into the ballroom." As I walk back inside, I can't stop thinking about Caesar. Does he like me or is it the alcohol talking?

A few dances later, I can't stand it. I have to find him, find out his true feelings. I go back into the lobby.

Caesar.

He grabs my arms and gently wraps them around his neck. He slides his arms around my waist.

"Come here," he says.

"I am here."

"Closer!"

"You're drunk, let me go."

I look in his eyes and see hurt. At that moment I swear he's sober. He kisses me.

I have never experienced a kiss like this one. Strange and wonderful, it is filled with passion. We pull apart. He smiles. It's clear he wants more.

I am only fourteen. I'm not ready for that. I am afraid someone, even Teresa, might see us. My head overrules my heart.

"No," I tell him.

He gets mad. He picks up a potted plant and throws it, breaking the pot. I look at him, hurt. He only wants one thing, I feel. I walk away and try to avoid him. Everywhere I look, his eyes follow me.

When it's time to leave, I slip out, unnoticed. I feel sad. What I did, though, I feel is for the best.

GRANDFATHER'S LAST REQUEST

There was no hospital in the town where my grandfather lived. He'd gone blind and had a fractured knee. He was home, in his bedroom. That day, a day after my fifteenth birthday, my grandfather had been thirsty.

He told me, *"Margarita, yo tengo deseo de una paleta. Por favor ve y cómprame una."*

I bought him the lollipop. He sucked on it, then gave it

back to me and shed one tear—a sign from God his death was near. Later when my mom felt his forehead, she started crying.

"El se está volviendo frío—cold," she said. *"Margarita, ve y dile a los familiares. Ve a la estación de radio también que lo anuncien."*

I did what she said. I told the relatives and asked the little radio station to announce the news. My grandfather was dead.

Some of the family ordered a casket. It had a small window in it so you could see his face. We dressed him in Levi's and a button-down shirt and put him in the casket on a table. The priest blessed him.

By five in the afternoon people started to gather. It is our tradition to have an all-night funeral. No one left until eight in the morning. They paid their last respects. They told my grandfather how much they loved him, gave him their kisses.

When I kissed him, I said, "I'm so sad we'll no longer sit together in the sun and talk of life."

I'm related to half the town and that morning all of them went to the funeral. Anyone could read a eulogy about him. Afterwards, we went to the cemetery. My grandfather was buried next to my grandmother and a great-aunt.

My mom wouldn't let go of the coffin.

CHRISTMAS BREAK, HEARTBREAK

After Christmas break, I'm sitting in my second-hour Spanish class—for native speakers. My mom speaks nothing but Spanish and wants me to take it. The teacher asks us to share something that happened to us during the vacation.

I write in my diary, "From this day forward, I swear to color all my days black."

I am hurt and bleeding, but I'm not going to let anyone know.

I build a wall around my emotions.

I pull back from my family, from Teresa.

I think about taking my life.

Sonia, my cousin, keeps trying to break through. "Talking will relieve you of what you're feeling. Trust me, Margarita. I won't tell anyone. I'm here for you, always."

The dam breaks and out flood my emotions. I cry. I tell her everything. "Caesar isn't anymore. Nothing will ever bring him back," she says. "Dwell on the good memories."

ONLY

That was the beginning of my healing. I practically memorized Michael Bolton's song, "When I'm Back on My Feet Again." Listening to it gave me the hope that I had lost.

I shouldn't have blocked my feelings. I should have talked to someone way before Sonia. I learned, too, that writing helped me have a better understanding of what happened.

Here's what I wrote last night: "It's been over a year since Teresa's *quinceañero* and Caesar's death. Teresa married and dropped out of school! At first I liked her husband, but now I hear he's abusing her.

"I never tire of looking at the pictures taken at her *quinceañero*. I still haven't visited Caesar's grave, though. I

This guy who sits across from me says a friend
on December 23rd, my birthday. I have a ba
"What's your friend's name?" I ask.

"Caesar."

My heart slams into my chest. I don't want to
"What happened?"

"Caesar and another guy were standing ou
dega," he says. "A car drives by and the people
shooting. Caesar dies instantly. The other is par

I am in shock as he continues his story.

Caesar was buried the same day as my gra
closed-coffin service. His little brother clung to
crying, "Why won't Caesar wake up? Why are
him at the cemetery?"

After class I find Teresa to tell her the story.
want to believe it, either. As she begins to cry
say, "Comfort her. She needs you."

I feel like screaming, "What about me?" In
calm, masking my feelings. When I get home,
"Did you hear about a drive-by shooting?"

"Yes," he tells me. "I didn't think it was imp
to mention. You were still grieving for your g

I run from the room, slam my bedroom doo
I have no tears left.

FLOOD OF EMOTIONS

In Mexico after my grandfather died, we wo
respect and memory of the person. I feel I o
to remember him. I will mourn him by wear

don't know if I can. Maybe one day I'll go and ask forgiveness.

"If only Caesar and I hadn't parted on bad terms. If only our feelings could have been spoken. If only. Never have there been words sadder than those."

DON'T GRIEVE FOR LONG

Cecil Begay, Counselor, Chinle Boarding School, Many Farms, Arizona

I am a Navajo. We are taught that if we live in harmony with ourselves, our environment and Mother Earth, we will reach old age. If we don't, one of these elements will take our life.

*

Unfortunately, Navajo teenagers are caught between two cultures: our own and the Anglo—the white culture. It's as though they are homeless children trying to survive.

Their parents can't help them. They don't know who else to turn to. Some turn to drugs, alcohol, suicide.

*

When students talk to me about death and life, I tell them, "Remember, in the Navajo way, death is always upon us. We have to learn how to deal with it."

*

THE HOLY PEOPLE

In our culture we try not to grieve for too long. We put our memories to rest. If we don't accept the death, it will hurt us.

After death the spirits are with the holy people. We live with these spirits all the time. They're watching us.

If the spirits come back to us too much in our dreams, that can be bad. Sometimes they come to give us warnings. Sometimes evil spirits come to haunt us. Right away we contact a medicine man. A special ceremony is done to cure us.

Sister

A PURE LOVE
Rasheeda, Age 16

My sister, Jasmine, suffered from Down syndrome. She was a lot older, nearly thirty. Because of Down, she had physical problems. She had a heart murmur. She had trouble eating, dressing, cleaning herself. And she wasn't able to communicate very well.

When she tried to speak, the words came out as mumbles. She could understand, though. If I asked her, "Jasmine, would you like to go to the store with me?" she showed signs that she knew.

About ten years ago, my mom started to travel in her work. She tried to keep Jasmine at home for as long as possible. Some of the people Mom found to care for Jasmine made fun of her.

My mom talked it over with my grandmother and they decided it was best to let Jasmine live in a special home. This was a school for people with problems such as Down syndrome. My grandmother often volunteered there.

We all went to visit her on weekends. Once when we were there, another girl began to have a seizure. My mother turned to me and said, "Rasheeda, honey, take Jasmine for a walk." Then she and my grandmother ran over to help the girl.

I took Jasmine and we walked hand in hand around the quad at school. That's such a strong remembrance for me.

It's hard to explain. With Jasmine I felt a pure love. It never got garbled with lies. Our love for each other was just there.

DIE IN PEACE

The doctor calls our house. He says to my mother, "Jasmine's heart has stopped beating. We've gotten it to go again. She's in the hospital, hooked up to a respirator."

This is critical, we know. We make constant trips back and forth, hoping things will get better. Jasmine doesn't respond to anything. She only breathes because of a life-support system.

After a week my mother says, "Turn off the machines. I want my daughter to die in peace."

A HAUNTING FEELING

My mother chose this absolutely gorgeous casket lined with white silk. Jasmine was in a pink shroud. My sister looked so pretty.

The funeral was small—a tug at the heart. All these years, few people acknowledged Jasmine, or took a moment to check on her. That made me feel resentful sometimes. By the time we got to the cemetery, I tried to push that thought out of my mind.

There were tourists around the day we laid Jasmine to rest. Here in New Orleans since the land's below sea level, the graves and tombstones are raised above the earth. Their shadows can be looming. People from up north like to take pictures of this.

To me death is a haunting feeling.

AFTERLIFE

I have a hard time believing in the concept of heaven and hell. I don't think that anybody's life can be judged good or bad.

I think you pass on to a better place. This world is so messed up that almost anything would be better. I just don't think there's someone making a choice about where you go.

I believe in reincarnation. Everybody comes back as another soul to re-do things we didn't have a chance to do before.

WAY TO GO

I'm African-American. When I die, I want what we call a second-line funeral. It's a music and dance celebration with African and Caribbean roots. The first half of the funeral is the mourning.

A jazz band—usually a drum, trumpet, trombone, and cymbals—starts out playing sad music to show our sorrow.

If it isn't too far, the band and mourners walk to the house of the person who's died. We knock on the front door, asking the soul to come out. We don't want it to haunt the house where it lived.

Then we proceed to the church. Throughout the ceremony, there's more mournful music. Afterwards as we walk to the cemetery, the music picks up. Once the person is laid to rest, it's time for a celebration!

There's New Orleans–style jazz and people doing this two-step dance right there in the cemetery. I think that's the way to go.

HEAVEN IS REAL

Pastor A. R. Bernard, Sr., *Christian Life Centre, Brooklyn, New York*

I tell the people in my congregation, "If you don't stand for something, you'll fall for everything."

*

We live our life in an "earth suit." That gives us the ability to communicate in this realm. Every human being has a purpose. After that purpose is fulfilled, we die. Death is the expiration of that earth suit, but it's not the cessation of life.

*

LAKE OF FIRE

For us death has more to do with separation. There are two forms of death in the Christian faith. There is the physical death, the separation of the spirit from the body. And there is the spiritual death, the separation from God.

Call it hell, call it the lake of fire, the bottom line is it's separation from God. Hell is the absence of all that is associated with God, goodness, faith, love, hope, security.

The torment of hell is remembering all the opportunities that you had to not be there.

To us a funeral is a joyous occasion. I call it a graduation service. We're moving from one realm to another. The aches and pains of life are no longer an issue. We rejoice because that person is rejoicing.

What they have lived by faith has now become their reality. They have passed through the veil of the flesh. Now they look back at us, cheering us on. "Heaven is real," they tell us. "Don't give up!"

Father

NO GOLF COURSES IN HEAVEN
Matthew, Age 17

At seven in the morning a drunk driver with no license hits my dad head-on. By the time my brothers and I, my sister, and my mother get to the hospital, he's losing it. He's in the intensive care unit with twenty tubes running in and out of his body.

I'm little then, second grade. I remember holding my dad's hand. It's warm. "I love you guys," he says to us. Ten seconds later his hand is ice cold. He's dead.

Nobody wants to believe it. The machine is, like, beep beep beeeeepp. I remember the sound. I remember it stops. A minute later it starts going again.

My sister freaks. *"He's alive!"* She's wrong. Once more the machine is quiet.

My dad dies on Good Friday, the same day that Christ died.

At the time I don't understand how permanent death is. I know he's not there right then. I don't know he won't be there the next week. When I figure that out, I'm mad. I feel abandoned.

LOVE AND CHICKEN POX

Every once in a while, now, ten years later, I really miss my dad. I'm not an emotional person. I'd just like to talk to him. Ask him what he thinks about my plans. What he thinks about how I'm doing now.

All the time I ask my mom and brothers and sister what Dad was like. Once when I was home sick with chicken pox, he drove an hour round trip to make me lunch.

I remember we'd go down to the park and play every sport: baseball, football, basketball, soccer. We'd be there five hours.

When we'd get home, he'd take a nap. I'd go into his bedroom and lie on his stomach. I thought he was the biggest person in the world.

Now I'm bigger than he was.

A HELLISH THING

My dad's death made me question my religion and my God. I wondered, "Why would Somebody that nice, forgiving, and merciful . . . take away my father?"

That's a hellish thing to do, especially when people are dependent on him.

I thought about that for a long time. Finally I came up with this theory. God's gifts include free will and individuality. If you're too dependent on a person, you lose your individuality. Maybe that's what happened to my mom. She was so dependent on my dad she lost herself.

Then God says, "Someone has to go," and He takes a person away.

Even though it's hard for me to fathom, I think you have

to believe there's something more. My sister, though, flat out thinks you rot in your grave.

Heaven is where you are with God. Hell is where God isn't.

There's no golf course in heaven. It's not like people are walking around. Instead, it's a huge conglomeration of souls. You're physically dead, but your brain's still working.

You can communicate, but you don't want to. You've reached your goal and you're happy with that. You're there for eternity.

FORCED TO GROW UP

A death in the family is horrible.

But I would not be the same person if my dad hadn't died.

I was forced to grow up. I know every valve and fuse in this house. When my friends are going to the beach, I'm home making screens for the windows. They would never think of doing that. I have to be responsible.

I learned where my place is—in the family. I learned how to make moral decisions. I think, "Well, what would Dad do in this situation?" That's my standard.

When I became a teenager, my mom and I were having some knock-down-drag-out fights. Then I thought, "I can't pull the wool over the eyes of a woman who's had three kids before me. Plus she can't talk this over with Dad. She's left here to deal with it."

I stopped arguing with her. It's not worth getting mad at each other. I'm probably more mature than most of my friends. They're still at the stage of throwing a tantrum, saying, "I'm gonna move out!"

MAMA'S BOY

All my best friends have asked me, "What's it like to have your father dead?"

I tell them, "I think it's hardest to lose a parent when you're a teenager."

When you're younger, you're kind of with your mother. In the middle ages, when you're a teenager, I think you need your father. You're looking for answers. Asking questions. When you get older, you have your own kid. You are a father and know most of the answers.

I don't tell my friends that when my dad died, I turned into a mama's boy. I never wanted to sleep at anyone's house. I didn't want to go away to swim camp.

There were times my mom would pick me up from Little League practice. She had tears in her eyes. She was still upset. So that night, maybe, I wouldn't go to my friend's house to look at baseball cards.

Now I think I was afraid. If I wasn't with my mom, she would leave me—die—the way my dad did. I would once more be abandoned.

THE PLAN

It's tough to lose a parent. What you can do, though, is take their memories and keep them with you. But you have to go on. If you dwell on the death, you're in trouble.

Think, "Wow, we had some wonderful times together."

Don't think, "Oh, he's dead."

Three, four, five years down the road, hopefully, you're not going to be that upset about it.

Sometimes even if your parent died a long time ago, the sadness comes back. You begin to have problems.

First think, "Does this go back to my parent's death?" If it does, figure out how you could make up for that loss somewhere else.

Maybe you could find the kind of relationship you had, but with somebody else—an uncle, a friend's parent, a neighbor. You don't have to ask the guy next door to go fishing with you, but you could go over there for a barbecue.

I think about how God plans things out. My dad died when I was seven. My mom still had to raise me. She didn't have time to totally concentrate on the death of my father.

This fall I'm going to leave for college. I was hesitant to go. I didn't want to leave my mother alone in this large house. But then my sister called up. She's going through a divorce. Could she and her two kids move in for a while? Everything seems to be working out.

NO HAY MAL QUE POR BIEN NO VENGA

Angela Jorge, Ph.D., *Professor, Hispanic Studies, State University of New York, Old Westbury, New York*

Cry when we're born, be joyous when we die.

*

GUARDIAN SPIRIT

In the Hispanic community—Puerto Rican, Cuban, Dominican, Mexican, and so on—many people are Catholics, and at the same time believe in spiritism. We believe that when individuals are born we are accompanied by a guardian spirit that stays with us through death.

The guardian helps the spirit of the person who's died disengage from the material world. For nine nights the family and friends say prayers. A white candle is lit, dedicated to that departing spirit.

We believe if we cry too much, if we are unwilling to accept God's will—the death of this person—we are pulling that spirit back to the material world. We want to allow it time to reintegrate into the spirit world. We want to let it be free.

Spiritists also believe in reincarnation. In each lifetime we're supposed to learn certain lessons. We're supposed to make contributions to humankind.

At death the spirit has to begin to understand what its mission was in the life that's just ended. Was the mission accomplished? What is left to be done? Together with God the spirit decides what will be the trials and tribulations of the next incarnation.

Then the spirit comes back again, reincarnated in another body. We have no guarantee we'll be the same sex or same racial group as the previous incarnation. With each successive incarnation, we are led toward the perfection of the spirit.

*

The death, the separation, is sad and difficult. We've been conditioned to feel that death isn't acceptable. We try to prolong life and postpone death.

Still, if we believe in spiritism, at the moment of our greatest pain, we tell ourselves: *"No hay mal que por bien no venga."* Out of every negative thing there is something positive. The spirit of a loved one is always with us.

WHERE THERE'S DEATH

. . . The study dealt with nearly 4,000 deaths of people over the age of 65. Heart disease, cancer, stroke and pneumonia lead the list of causes. Thirty percent of the people died in their homes, 45 percent in the hospital and 25 percent in a nursing home. More than half died peacefully in their sleep.

[*New York Newsday* 8/27/91]

Their Death,
Your Life

A NEXT STEP

I started out writing this book for you. Teenagers had told me coping with death was a topic that interested them. I finished writing it for you and for myself, too. Doing the book became part of my own healing.

*

In October my friend Andrea was diagnosed with liver cancer. Our birthdays are a week apart. We talk on the phone almost every day. In these past few months, she's had surgery, chemotherapy, and mixed news.

We're learning how to talk about what she's going through. We both have a hard time even saying the word "death" to each other.

*

Then one afternoon while I was in Los Angeles on business, partway through this book's research and writing, I was finally forced to look death in the eye.

I didn't see it coming.

*

TRIGGER DECISION

In a fancy hotel room, a man pretending he'd been sent to check on a leak, a man twice my size, stuck a gun in my face and said, "Lie down on the bed or I'll kill you."

In my mind's eye I "saw" the explosion the gun made when he pulled the trigger. I "saw" my own death.

I thought about the family and friends I'd leave behind. I thought about how they would mourn me, how their lives would go on without me. I realized I'd never know what they'd do. This was my life; that would be theirs.

I realized, too, that no matter what I did, whether or not that man killed me was his decision.

My decision was to resist.

I reasoned with him, reminding him I was a human being. When that made no difference, I fought back. I screamed. He fractured my cheek with his gun, left me bleeding and in shock.

In the end he took my money, but not my life.

In the weeks that followed, I spent a lot of time thinking about Andrea and me, and trying to make sense of it all.

Then I began to really listen to the advice I was hearing from those who speak on these pages. And you know what? What worked for them is working for me, and maybe can work for you. Why not give it a try?

Some of you live with such a level of violence in your world that when someone dies, the goal of healing yourself is that much harder to achieve.

But it's not impossible.

You have to accept these lessons: Random violence is meaningless. Death isn't. As you've learned through this book, death is part of life. You can't make sense of violence. You can make sense of death.

*

SURVIVAL LESSONS

To survive the death of someone special, you should talk and talk and talk about these issues. Write, sing, dance, run, and scream out your feelings.

Remember, there's always someone to listen, someone to help you. Reach out.

Then let go of the pain. In tribute to the loved one who's died, grieve and move on.

You've taken a first step by reading this book. Now take a next step. Think about your priorities and your values. What's important to you? Make this a time to plan for your future. Let death be a lesson about life. Let it be life-affirming.

NOTE: If you have any comments about death in your life, please write me:
Janet Bode
c/o Delacorte Press
1540 Broadway
New York, New York 10036

WITH THANKS

During the year I spent researching and writing this book, my family and friends offered continual support.

Thanks go to my family: the Bodes, Barbara and Carolyn; the Macks, Pearl, Kenny, and Peter; the Lutzes, Frieda and Ernie. And my friends, Lucy Cefalu, Jeanne Dougherty, Kay Franey, Jean Furukawa, Ted Gottfried, Carole Mayedo, Marvin Mazor, Rosemarie Mazor, Joe Mohbat, Judy Pollock, Michael Sexton, Rafael Sidauy, and the Third Thursday Writers Group.

The following people provided me with invaluable assistance:

California: Kenyon Chan, Chair, Asian Studies Department, University of California at Northridge; and Sally Lahm, Research Fellow, Wildlife Conservation International, San Diego and Makokou, Gabon, Africa.

Colorado: Owen Blacklock, Professor of Psychology, Western State College, Gunnison.

Florida: Michael Lunskis, Media Specialist, Island Branch Library, Holmes Beach.

Indiana: Mara Becking, Media Specialist, and Beverly Hubbs, Counselor, Chesterton High School, Chesterton.

Iowa: Kathleen Bognanni, Media Specialist, Franklin Branch Library, Des Moines; Jim Carnahan, Counselor, South Alternative High School, Des Moines; Matt Kollasch, Media Specialist, Cedar Falls High School, Cedar Falls; and Jan Leise, Media Specialist, and Carol White, Counselor, Lincoln High School, Des Moines.

Louisiana: Cathleen Friedmann, Media Specialist, Park Country Day School, Metairie.

New Mexico: Duane Blue Spruce, Institute of American Indian Arts, Santa Fe; and Rebecca Maldonado, Director, Title IV Program, Santa Fe.

New York: Glenda Phipps, Literacy Teacher, Mott Haven Library, Bronx; Amy Wagner, Sparks Counselor, Lower East Side Prep, New York.

Ohio: Debbie Fullhart, Media Specialist, Southview High School, Sylvania; Peggy Rabideau, Media Specialist, Sylvania School District, Sylvania.

Tennessee: Lurlene McDaniel, Writer, Chattanooga.

Utah: Sharren Matthews, Media Specialist, and Chris Young, Teacher, West High School, Salt Lake City.

Wisconsin: Sue Dennis, Media Specialist, South High School, Sheboygan; Kathy Fisher, Journalism Teacher, and Jane Shoemaker, Media Specialist, North High School, Sheboygan.

And, of course, a special thank-you to the individual teenagers who volunteered to share their stories. If they hadn't been willing to open their lives, this book would not exist.

NOTES

DEATH IS NOT OPTIONAL

1. Warren E. Leary, "Not Even Death Ends Anti-Pollution Crusade," *New York Times, 8/27/91,* Science Section.

2. National Adolescent Health Survey, 1987, conducted by U.S. Public Health Service. Researchers surveyed 11,419 eighth- and tenth-graders from twenty states. Some findings related to potential of death:

56 percent of teens surveyed said they hadn't worn a seat belt the last time they rode in a car.

46 percent of tenth-graders and 18 percent of eighth-graders said the last time they were in a car, the driver had used alcohol or drugs.

18 percent of teen females and 11 percent of teen males had tried to kill themselves.

64 percent of the males and 19 percent of the females had used a gun in the past year.

50 percent of the males and 28 percent of the females said they had had a fight where they were physically attacked. Physical fighting is the number-one cause that leads to homicide.

Study conducted by the Annie E. Casey Foundation and the Center for the Study of Social Policy, released 3/23/92. Nationwide the violent death rate of teenagers between fifteen and nineteen years old increased 11 percent. This was led by a rise in suicides and homicides. [Years studied, 1984–89, were the most recent available.]

BOOKS

Sharing grief and loss eases the pain. Maybe you want to talk with a parent or trusted adult, but don't know how to start. Pick up one of Earl Grollman's many books, such as *Talking About Death: A Dialogue Between Parent and Child* (Boston: Beacon Press, 1976) or *What Helped When My Loved One Died* (Boston: Beacon Press, 1981). These are meant to be shared.

When the death is a parent's, you could check out Jill Krementz's book *How It Feels When a Parent Dies* (New York: Alfred A. Knopf, 1982). Eighteen students ages seven to sixteen, half of them teenagers, talk about loss and survival. Eda LeShan's book *Learning to Say Good-bye: When a Parent Dies* (New York: Macmillan, 1976; Avon, 1978) is good, too.

Maybe your little sister or brother is having trouble facing the death of a loved one. Together you could read Judith Viorst's picture book *The Tenth Good Thing About Barney* (New York: Atheneum, 1971; Aladdin Books, 1975).

If you're working on a paper on this topic, you might begin your research with a book by Elisabeth Kübler-Ross. Many consider *On Death and Dying* (New York: Macmillan, 1969) her most important. You could also read *Living with Death and Dying* (New York: Collier Books, 1981).

Depending on your assignment, you could check your library for *Death and Afterlife,* Stephen T. Davis, editor (New York: St. Martin's Press, 1989); *The Wisdom of the Serpent: The Myths of Death, Rebirth and Resurrection,* by Joseph L. Henderson and Maud Oakes (Princeton, NJ: Princeton University Press, 1990); *Encyclopedia of Death,* Robert and Beatrice Kastenbaum, editors (Phoenix: Oryx Press, 1989); and *Endings: A Sociology of Death and Dying,* by Michael C. Kearl (New York: Oxford University Press, 1989).

Reading novels in which people confront loss might help you examine your own grief. In Louisa May Alcott's classic *Little Women* (originally published in 1869, now New York: Macmillan, 1962), Beth, her family, and friends must deal with her illness and eventual death.

Lurlene McDaniel writes thoughtful teen novels which concern death. Her titles include *Goodbye Doesn't Mean Forever* (New York: Bantam Books, 1989), *Too Young to Die* (New York: Bantam Books, 1989), *Somewhere Between Life and Death* (New York: Bantam Books, 1991), the One Last Wish series (New York: Bantam Books, 1992), and *Six Months to Live* (Pinellas Park, FL: Willowisp Press, 1985). You also might read Russell Banks's *The Sweet Hereafter* (New York: HarperCollins, 1991), a gripping story in which fourteen kids are killed in a school bus accident.

VIDEOS

Many movies available on videotape focus on coping with death, as well as coping with violence. Some to consider are *Ordinary People*, *Dead Poets Society*, *Boyz 'N the Hood*, *Thunderheart*, and *Truly, Madly, Deeply*.